Family
gardens

THE ROYAL HORTICULTURAL SOCIETY

Family gardens

Lia Leendertz

LONDON, NEW YORK, MUNICH, MELBOURNE, DELHI

PROJECT EDITOR Emma Callery
PROJECT ART EDITOR Alison Shackleton
SENIOR EDITOR Helen Fewster
MANAGING ART EDITOR Alison Donovan
PICTURE RESEARCH Lucy Claxton, Mel Watson
PRODUCTION EDITOR Kavita Varma
US EDITOR Jenny Siklos

PHOTOGRAPHY Peter Anderson

First American Edition, 2008

Published in the United States by
DK Publishing 375 Hudson Street
New York, New York 10014

08 09 10 11   10 9 8 7 6 5 4 3 2 1

[RD146—March 09]

A catalog record for this book is available
from the Library of Congress.

ISBN 978-0-7566-4269-3

Printed and bound by Star Standard Industries Pte. Ltd., Singapore

DK books are available at special discounts when purchased in
bulk for sales promotions, premiums, fund-raising, or
educational use. For details, contact: DK Publishing Special
Markets, 375 Hudson Street, New York, New York 10014 or
SpecialSales@dk.com.

Discover more at
www.dk.com

Contents

Lia Leendertz is a gardening writer and
mother of two young children. She has a community
garden plot and a home-based garden and lives in
Bristol, England. A regular contributor to *The
Garden* and other gardening magazines, she also
has a weekly gardening question and answer
column in London's *The Guardian* newspaper.

Inspiring family yards

The family yard is the place where you and your family can play and relax together. It may well be a refuge from the outside world, but most importantly, it is a place where the whole family feels at home. Some family yards are straightforward play areas, for allowing little ones to let off steam during the day, while others come alive at night, when children are sleeping and friends come to visit. Perhaps you want to produce fresh fruit and vegetables for family meals, or make it a place to learn about wildlife. Find the features that most appeal to you.

Play areas

For families with young children, the opportunities a back yard provides for outdoor play become the most important aspect of the yard. With a little imagination, play areas can be beautiful as well as fun.

Pictures clockwise from far left

Play garden An area dedicated to play can also be filled with plants. Sturdy climbing apparatus and rope swings are always popular, but there is no reason why such features can't also be used for climbing plants, such as clematis, or emerge from a bed of attractive foliage plants. Use bedding plants to etch out nursery-scale numbers or to form the pattern on a mythical creature. Brightly colored perennials surrounding a play area will give pleasure to adults and children alike.

Playhouse and slide A playhouse gives children somewhere they can escape into their own little world. Those on stilts have some of the other-worldly properties of a treehouse. A playhouse close to the main house and surrounded by stark lawn does not feel very private, and is unlikely to be well used, but nestled among plantings, it blends into the garden and becomes a far more attractive destination. Careful pruning to ensure children always have a clear sightline of home will make them feel secure despite being hidden.

Flower maze Mazes and labyrinths invite children into them again and again and are an excellent focus for a large lawn or expanse of patio. Mazes have several routes to find the center; labyrinths have only one path to be followed. Both are equally appealing to adults and children alike. A labyrinth or maze can be a permanent feature, when made from pavers or of gravel-filled channels in grass. But they can also be temporary, made from daffodils that disappear later in the season, mown out of long grass, or even created with rope for a special occasion, such as a birthday party.

Sandbox This sandbox replaced a pool when young children moved to the garden. Surrounded by sweet smelling herbs, such as lavender, the area is perfect for quiet play. The planting shields the buckets and spades from the adult seating area.

Outdoor living

The most successful family back yards offer space for everyone to enjoy: a place for children to play, somewhere to cook and eat outside, and an area to unwind and relax in the evening.

Pictures clockwise from top left

Secluded hide-away Design an area where you and the children can relax and take time to talk or read. This pretty arbor seat is ideal, and offers a cool, shady spot from which to enjoy the sights and sounds of the yard.

Outdoor fireplace This vibrant yellow outdoor fireplace creates a wonderful focal point and warm homely atmosphere for evening gatherings, while also lending the garden a bold, contemporary look.

Hammock A hammock may well be the perfect place to unwind alone with a book in a shady part of the yard, but there is no denying that it can also be a lot of fun, doubling as an impromptu piece of play equipment. It will be popular with every member of the family.

Barbeque No back yard would be complete without somewhere to cook outdoors. A brick-built barbeque in a corner of a patio that is always there, ready to be fired up, will get more use than one that needs to be brought out from storage each time you want to use it.

Encouraging wildlife

Your back yard will have more interest if it is a home to wildlife as well as your family. The comings and goings of birds and other creatures are fascinating and a child's garden that is full of wildlife may inspire a lifelong passion for nature.

Pictures clockwise from far left

Pond Wildlife ponds are always buzzing with life. They create homes and breeding places for frogs, newts, and dragonflies, and all manner of creatures visit and make use of them at some stage in their life cycle.

Nesting box A nesting box, positioned against a tree or wall in a sheltered spot, provides a safe home where birds can raise their families. If you are lucky, you may get visited by the same breeding pair over several years, and there will always be a succession of young birds using your yard. Position them near a food source or in an area of wild planting, and the parents and fledglings will never have too far to go for a meal.

Path through long grass A wildlife garden need not be messy. If the thought of leaving grass long worries you, you can make it look neat and deliberate by mowing a definite edge to an area. Here, an arrow-straight path cuts through a swathe of long grass and wild flowers, leaving no doubt that this is a well-managed area.

Bird bath Food and shelter are important for birds, but water is often overlooked. It can be in short supply for birds both in the heat of summer and during winter frosts, so keep a year-round supply and you will have year-round visitors. A bird bath full of water is an attractive garden feature in its own right.

Wild flowers If you have the space, there is nothing that is more romantic than an area of nectar-rich meadow filled with pollinating insects. To create such an environment, choose natural wild flower mixes or a more ornamental and colorful mix (*see pp.88–89*).

Sensory gardens and yards

The sensory qualities of your yard can create an adventure for little hands, noses, and mouths. Yards rich in such detail also appeal to those who struggle with their sight or hearing.

Pictures clockwise from top left

Wind chimes Audible garden features can be plants with stems that knock or swish together, or they can be simple devices such as wind chimes. Those made from metal make a tinkling sound, while the sound made by wooden chimes is more subtle and earthy.

Herbs A herb garden is a joy to the senses, particularly those of scent and taste. Herb seats and herb borders that are brushed against as you walk release scent on contact. Many herbs can be eaten raw, and you can enjoy their strong, zingy tastes as you walk around the garden.

Furry plants There are many plants that are appealing to the touch at some stage in their life cycle. *Clematis tangutica* may be grown for its show of yellow flowers, but it then has a tactile display of soft, silky seedheads.

Seedheads Some plants are made for the sensory garden. As well as looking unusual, the seedheads of *Scabiosa stellata* are irresistibly tactile and audible, making a satisfying papery noise when touched.

Creating privacy

No matter how much you love your family, or how friendly your neighbors are, there are times when you want some privacy. A yard is more enjoyable if there is a sense that it is a place where you can escape the rest of the world.

Pictures clockwise from top left

Summer house A summer house is a major structure in the yard, and it creates an indoor space divorced from the house. It could be used as a private and peaceful office or studio that allows you to work quietly, away from the hustle and bustle of family life. Alternatively, it can be a place for teenagers to find the privacy they crave. If you have no other use for a summer house, it makes an excellent spot in which to sit and enjoy the yard during a rainstorm.

Hedge dividers A yard that has no internal divisions lacks mystery: everything and everyone in it can be seen at a glance. By positioning a series of hedges within the garden, you create intrigue and allow yourself to become lost. While this works well on a grand scale it is just as applicable to smaller yards and would be a particularly good solution in smaller urban yards, creating a series of small garden rooms.

Privacy from being overlooked In many urban areas, your yard is likely to be overlooked from the windows of your neighbors. Even just a simple umbrella can provide that small barrier that prevents you from feeling that everyone around can watch what you are doing.
A pergola densely covered with climbing plants is a more permanent solution to the same problem. Similarly, planting trees that will eventually arch their limbs over your yard can make the yard feel much more private in the longer term.

Improvized hideaway A simple cone of climbers makes a flowery bower, perfect as a hideaway for any child. This version relies on supports made into a cone shape and then planted up in spring, but in winter you could make an equally effective, albeit more permanent, version by pushing willow stalks into the ground in a circle and tying them together at the top. They will leap into life and the structure becomes covered in greenery in spring.

The vegetable patch

There are few better favors you can do for your family than to encourage an interest in vegetable growing. Having a vegetable garden or plot means your children will be eating the freshest of vegetables, and plenty of them, too.

Pictures clockwise from left

Vegetable garden A vegetable garden brimful of produce can be a beautiful sight. There is no reason that vegetable gardens shouldn't be attractive as well as productive: the textures of crinkly lettuce leaves and feathery carrot tops next to the blue-green of a brassica leaf and a splash of color from an edible flower make a tapestry of textures and colors as lovely as in any ornamental garden. Hard-landscaped paths or small border hedges will keep it looking good during the quieter times.

Fruit trees Every garden, no matter how small, should have a fruit tree. Many fruit trees thrive on being trained and pruned into the sort of shapes that suit the smaller garden. Apples, pears, cherries, and peaches can all be trained against a wall, taking up almost no space. The harder you prune fruit trees, and the less you allow them to put their energy into growth, the more they will concentrate on producing lots of fruit year on year.

Herbs Culinary herbs are compact and atractive, and easy to fit in among ornamental plantings or vegetables. Some, such as chives, make great edging plants for vegetable beds. Others are particularly ornamental: fennel has delicate, wispy growth and can be grown through a border of colorful plants. Gather a collection of commonly used culinary herbs—basil, oregano, mint—in containers by the kitchen door, to allow you to reach them quickly, even when it is raining or cold.

Produce Make a list of all of the vegetables that your family eat regularly and find out how to grow them. Some may be impossible in your climate, but others, such as tomatoes, are relatively easy to grow and from late summer will produce all the fruits you can eat, plus more. Start off with a few easy crops, such as tomatoes, carrots, and salad leaves, and see where your interest takes you.

Outdoor play

Toddlers don't have the monopoly on fun in the yard. It should be a place where we can all get excercise, expend excess energy, and relieve stress, no matter what our age.

Pictures clockwise from top left

Treehouse It may be hard to get some children to get exercise, but it is usually easy to get them to play. A treehouse may be the ultimate den, and the perfect spot for fantasy play, but just by getting into and out of it children will be building up their fitness, while having no idea that they are doing something that is good for them. A ladder up to a height demands concentration, balance, and nerves of steel. The addition of a rope walk and a rope swing turns just an hour or two of play into a major mental and physical workout, and all while they are out in the fresh air, too.

Swings A natural feature, such as this dead tree, will win out over even the most sophisticated piece of play equipment. Tree climbing should be a part of every childhood, but opportunities for this fun, natural activity are scarce. A tree can be climbed over and ropes and swings can be hung from it. This one even has buckets of bedding plants attached to its branches. This yard has been made yet more appealing with a willow den for private games, and a hammock for young children to swing in and for older children and adults to relax in.

Chess An oversized chess set makes a striking feature, the black-and-white sculptural pieces making it particularly suitable for a modern or minimalist yard with plenty of hard landscaping, or for a square of a well-kept lawn. Chess is not an obvious party game, but there are many other oversized yard games available that have been designed with outdoor gatherings in mind.

Fitness logs You don't have to buy lots of expensive exercise equipment to keep the children amused. These wooden logs have been designed to act as a simple obstacle course for little kids to enjoy, and they also make an attractive natural feature in the flower garden. They have been cut long and then part of their length set into the ground for stability. Once securely in place, they have been surrounded by a thick layer of bark chippings to soften any falls.

Getting started

A family yard is not just for children. The yard can be designed so that every member of the family—young or old, and even the family pet—is drawn to spend time there. Think about what each member of your family needs from a yard before you start laying it out. Then, once you have made these decisions, there are a number of practical choices to be made. Will you go for hard or soft surfaces? Which plants will be most appropriate? How can the space accommodate animals? This section guides you through the options for your family's needs.

Planning your backyard

Before you start laying out your backyard, think about the individual members of your family and the features they might particularly enjoy.

Family space This design includes dedicated play and eating areas as well as low-maintenance planting. Clever design and vibrant color make it feel modern and lively—a place to relax and play in.

For a young family

Play is likely to be at the top of any young family's list, and you may want to consider a number of different features that will keep young minds entertained.

Play equipment Swings and slides can be situated in their own area, if you have space, or integrated into the yard, with a little ingenuity. Some swing seats can later be turned into arbors, and rope swings from trees are easily moved when children lose interest.

Water and sand play Sand pits and paddling pools provide young children with hours of fun. Paddling pools in particular will be most used on hot days, so make sure you have an area of dappled shade in which to site them. They should also be close to the house for safety.

Storage Toys can take over a yard. Make sure you can stow them away at the end of a day's play (*see pp.108–109*).

For older children

Backyard needs change as children get older. Some will become more physical and need larger, sturdier play equipment, some want to lounge on the lawn, while others just want to be alone.

Privacy Older children are most likely to use the yard if they feel they have space and facilities to do their own thing. A den or treehouse is perfect for this.

Fun and exercise Features such as a hot tub or a trampoline will encourage teenagers to spend time in the yard with friends. For safety, a trampoline can be sunk into the ground or it can be encircled by a net.

Lawn A lawn may be great for toddlers to stumble around on, but becomes even more useful as children grow up. There is no better place for playing soccer, picnicing, or even just sunbathing.

Planning your yard *continued*

For adults

It is easy to overlook your own needs in the yard in favor of those of children. Make sure the yard has plenty of features for you too.

Greenhouse Many people find that an interest in gardening develops as their children grow older and they have more time on their hands. A greenhouse allows you to propagate vegetables and ornamental plants and extend the season for vegetable growing. If you are interested in propagating, consider a cold frame, too, for hardening off seedlings.

Entertaining areas Create a comfortable seating area in the yard with plenty of atmospheric night lighting where you can enjoy evenings with friends or time alone during the day. An awning provides some shelter from the elements, and makes this an even more inviting space.

For the elderly

Older people have different needs in their yard, and may wish to make it low-maintenance so that they can continue to enjoy it, rather than having it turn into a chore.

Paths and planting Large lawns should be the first thing to go if you are struggling to keep up your yard. Wide, level paths surrounded by planting are far easier to look after. Choose evergreen plants with interesting foliage, rather than relying on maintenance-heavy flowering perennials, and get plenty of mulch in between to keep the weeds at bay.

Wildlife Encouraging a variety of wildlife can make spending time in the yard even more enjoyable. Site bird feeders and baths where you can easily see them from the house or a patio. Squirrels, chipmunks, frogs, toads, and butterflies could all become regular visitors.

For the disabled

Access to the yard can be a frustrating problem for some disabled people, but there are ways of bringing the yard to you, through hard landscaping and carefully thought out planting.

Hard landscaping For the wheelchair-bound and those with reduced mobility, raised beds are a great feature, allowing you to reach into beds to weed, plant, and water, or simply to get closer to the plants in order to enjoy them. Sturdy ramps will help you to move around any changes of level in the yard.

Sensory planting Your yard and gardens shouldn't just look good. Those with poor eyesight may enjoy planting up a sensory garden, which includes plants with particularly tactile leaves and seedheads, a beautiful or unusual scent, or those that make a noise when they are touched or blown by the wind.

Lawns and alternative surfaces

The surfaces you use in your yard —both hard and soft—will depend on the amount of time that you have available for maintaining them as well as the individual needs of your family.

Grass A lawn is attractive and durable and perfect for young families, but it needs a lot of maintenance. In summer it needs cutting every week—not a great option for those short on time or less physically able.

Tiles Well-laid tiles can be a good choice for the elderly, as it is level and easy to navigate, but be sure to choose something that is not slippery after rain. Families with toddlers may find tiles a problem.

Gravel Gravel is cheap and instant, but is not a good surface for areas where you want to place tables and chairs. It is most useful for surrounding a small level patio or a series of stepping stones.

Decking Wood decking is warm and inviting for small bare feet, and smooth and level for the elderly. Building a deck is one of the easiest ways to create a sophisticated living and dining area close to the house.

Boundaries

The boundaries of your yard can be treated in a number of different ways to different effect. You can also use boundaries within the yard to hide certain ugly or messy features or to create separate areas that will look distinct and feel private from the rest of the yard. They can be useful for creating shade, too.

Covering wire fences Wire fences may look ugly, but they are easily covered with quick growing annual or perennial climbers. They are also very thin, even when covered in plants, and so make excellent screens for a less ornamental area of the yard, such as the compost bins.

Espaliered pear on wall A large south-facing wall is the perfect growing spot for many plants and should never be left bare. Here a pear has been trained along the wall, and the heat of the wall will help fruit to ripen early.

Clipped hedging around bench Low box hedging will never prevent the determined from crossing it, but it is a strong visual statement that may discourage children from straying onto plantings or into other no-go areas.

Artistic fencing You may wish to draw attention to your boundaries, rather than trying to hide them. This artistic space uses bold paint colors and sculpture to make the fence itself into a piece of art.

Hedge as planting backdrop A well-clipped hedge is a great backdrop for a colorful border. This combination takes a lot of maintenance, however, so may not be suitable for the elderly or those with young children.

Planting along wall One of the best ways to make your space seem bigger than it really is, is to disguise the boundaries by planting trees and shrubs. This also helps to create privacy from neighbors.

Raised beds

Raised beds have a place in many family gardens: they make great designated children's beds, but also enable the elderly and disabled to continue gardening.

Logs with sitting areas Here, logs have been used not only to make raised beds, but as a retaining wall for coping with a change in level. This makes a useful and productive space out of a tricky slope.

Bricks If you want a permanent and low-maintainance raised bed, have one built for you out of brick. They can be made fairly tall for particularly easy access and, once in place, will last for many years.

Sleepers Railway sleepers also make sturdy raised beds, simply stacked on top of each other and pinned in place. Most are wide enough to be used as a seat; useful if you cannot stand for long.

Shallow A raised bed doesn't have to be a large landscaped feature. Even just a shallow bed can be easier to maintain than the surrounding soil. It should be regularly topped up with compost.

Wicker A woven wicker edge makes an attractive raised bed for herbs or flowers. This is a fairly temporary solution, though, as the wicker will eventually rot away from contact with damp soil.

Features for wildlife

Many wild creatures rely on backyards for both shelter and food, and you will get a great deal of enjoyment from welcoming and encouraging them into yours.

Bird nesting box A bird nesting box provides a secure home for birds and their young. This quirky version sits on top of an obelisk, and will soon be made more private and appealing by the growing foliage.

Bird feeders Place a variety of feeders around the yard to appeal to different types of birds. This is a ground-feeding feeder. It will encourage ground-feeding birds such as doves and finches. Not good if you have squirrels!

Flowers for butterflies Flowers that are rich in nectar will be attractive to butterflies. Encourage them by planting some in a sunny place sheltered from winds and provide wet sand from which they can take a drink.

Log pile A log pile provides a home for beetles and frogs, and can even make a winter shelter for a chipmunk or weasel. Leave a few piles undisturbed in nooks of the yard to tempt in these beneficial creatures.

Insect house Insect houses act as winter quarters for beneficial creatures such as native bees, ladybugs, and lacewings. Site them near plants that are attacked by aphids, so they can get right to work in the spring.

Choosing plants

Through careful plant choice you can have a yard that is designed either to withstand the attentions of lively children, to be easy to maintain, to give quick results, or to include a strong sensory interest.

Sturdy plants

Yards and gardens that are home to energetic children need plants that can put up with a bit of abuse. There is no use in planting a border of delicate flowers if you are going to get upset every time they get hit by a football.

Tough and pliable It is possible to fill your yard only with plants that have strong growth and pliable stems, that will bend when hit, rather than snap, or that recover from breakages quickly. Such plants may not be the most exciting of choices, but they will at least clothe your yard in greenery for the relatively short period when they are under attack. Later on they can be swapped for more exciting plants.

Border edgings If you are determined to hang on to your flower border, you can use plants to shield it from straying children. A hedge of short-growing plants will deflect the worst, but you will nevertheless have to resign yourself to occasional casualties.

Many plants recover quickly from blows, but you will have to prune out dead growth to ensure that they continue to thrive.

Choice of plant Here is a selection of sturdy plants, some of which make good border edgings. Those such as *Cotoneaster horizontalis* are incredibly tough and you would have to try pretty hard to make much impact on them. Cordylines form strong, treelike trunks and grasses, such as *Carex flagelliera*, have such light, pliable leaves that they spring back into shape after being stepped on or hit—just what is needed for the family garden.

- *Artemisia schmidtiana* "Nana"
- *Bergenia*
- *Buxus sempervirens*
- *Carex flagellifera*
- *Cordyline australis*
- *Cotoneaster horizontalis*
- *Hakonechloa macra* "Aureola"
- *Hebe* "Red Edge"
- *Liriope muscari*
- *Mahonia* x *media* "Charity"
- *Miscanthus sinensis* "Gracillimus"
- *Nandina domestica*
- *Phyllostachys nigra*
- *Sarcococca confusa*
- *Stipa tenuissima*
- *Trachycarpus fortunei*

| *Cordyline australis* | *Cotoneaster horizontalis* | *Carex flagellifera* | *Phyllostachys nigra* |

Low-maintenance plants

As we get older and less mobile, it makes sense to plant things that will look after themselves for most of the year, and not require a lot of pruning or fussing over. You may have a young family or a busy job and so have little time for maintenance and just want to be able to enjoy the yard without feeling guilty about the work to be done.

Plants If you want to keep things low maintenance, you will not have the full gamut of plants to choose from. Learn to love foliage, and forsake some flowers. For instance, annual bedding and perennial borders are among the most time-intensive ways of gardening.

Surfaces Lawns take up a huge amount of time. They need mowing regularly, and have a fall and spring maintenance regime of fertilizing, scratching out dead grass, and aerating. If you can do without one, you will make your life a lot easier.

Care Weeding and watering are among the most time-consuming elements of yard and garden care. Before planting, lay a weed-suppressing cloth. Cut holes to plant through it and then cover with mulch to keep moisture in. It takes more initial work than simply planting, but you will save yourself time in the long run.

Slate chippings on the surface of the soil look good and cut down on weeding and watering.

Choice of plants Low-maintenance plants generally look after themselves, and look good even if they are slightly neglected. Slow-growing evergreens and conifers are among the easiest to look after, once they are established, as they simply grow slightly larger each year. There are a few flowering plants, such as hardy geraniums and fuchsias, that qualify as low maintenance as they flower over a long season with so little input.

- *Anemone hupehensis* var. *japonica*
- *Aucuba japonica* "Crotonifolia"
- *Berberis darwinii*
- *Choisya ternata* Sundance
- *Euonymus fortunei* "Silver Queen"
- *Fatsia japonica*
- *Fuchsia* "Mrs. Popple"
- *Geranium himalayense* "Gravetye"
- *Hebe cupressoides* "Boughton Dome"
- *Phormium* "Sundowner"
- *Picea glauca* var. *albertiana* "Conica"
- *Sedum* Autumn Joy
- *Yucca filamentosa*

| *Fuchsia* "Mrs. Popple" | *Phormium* "Sundowner" | *Geranium himalayense* | *Anemone hupehensis* |

Choosing plants *continued*

Plants for quick results

Young children have short attention spans, so to get them interested in gardening, choose plants that do something spectacular, fast. While no plant gives instant results, many germinate and turn into something recognizable quickly enough for your child to remember sowing them.

Annuals Annuals germinate, grow, flower, and seed within one year, and this quick turn around makes them appealing to children. There are many annuals that are suitable for the community garden plot or vegetable bed, but also a number that will produce very pretty flowers. Annual climbers, such as sweet pea (*Lathyrus odoratus*) and black-eyed Susan (*Thunbergia alata*), have particularly rapid growth, and can cover a fence in a season.

Bulbs Bulbs do not give instant results but they are pretty quick and incredibly simple to grow—a child will certainly have the attention span to dig a hole, push in a bulb and cover it. Seeing the shoots of a bulb they have planted emerging from the ground in spring is a magical experience for a child, and enough to get many hooked.

Sprouts For the quickest possible results, grow some seed sprouts in a jar. This will demonstrate germination to little ones, and create some delicious salad ingredients.

When growing annual bedding plants, keep them fed and watered if you want them to grow fast and flower well.

Choice of plants Sunflowers (*Helianthus*) are a great choice for first seed sowing, as they are quick growing and so bold and colorful once they are flowering. Climbers such as *Ipomoea* are another quick and colorful choice. Edible crops should be picked and eaten when they are young and sweet. Children might even be tempted to try lettuce if it is young and fresh enough, and they have sown the seed themselves.

- *Calendula*
- *Centaurea*
- *Cosmos*
- *Eschscholzia californica*
- *Helianthus*

- *Hyacinthus* "Woodstock"
- *Ipomoea*
- *Lathyrus odoratus*
- *Narcissus* "Tête-à-tête"
- *Tulipa* "Prinses Irene"

- Green beans
- Carrots
- Zucchini
- Cress
- Lettuce

- New potatoes
- Pumpkins
- Strawberries
- Sugar snap peas
- Sweetcorn

| *Helianthus* | *Ipomoea purpurea* | Zucchini | Lettuce |

Sensory planting

All gardens are sensory gardens to a certain extent, but a specially planted sensory garden will have been designed to heighten the experience of all of the senses, rather than concentrating primarily on sight. They may have been made to appeal to those with poor or no eyesight, but will greatly appeal to children as well.

Scent A sensory garden should be filled with scent, so the visitor is aware of being in a well-planted place without even needing to touch the plants. As well as an overall pleasant fragrance, include plants with more piquant smells, such as mints and thyme.

Sound Many plants rustle when touched or are blown by the wind, or make knocking or swishing noises when brushing against themselves. To increase the sense of sound, add wooden sticks to bang together and wind chimes to blow in the breeze.

Touch There are lots of plants that are soft to the touch, but also many that invite you to stroke them because of shiny bark or papery seed heads. Children don't usually need telling to reach out and touch the more tactile plants in a garden, but it is good to create a place where they can be encouraged to do so.

Harvesting seeds allows children to get hold of and manipulate plants and feel their different textures.

Choice of plants Honeysuckle (*Lonicera*) spreads its honey scent all around, but you could also include plants that appeal specifically to children's sense of smell, such as the delicious chocolate cosmos (*C. atrosanguineus*). Place it next to a mint for a juxtaposition of warm and cool fragrances. Plant tactile plants, such as papery *Physalis alkekengi* and fuzzy *Stachys byzantina* "Big Ears," next to paths and scented plants on raised beds at nose level.

- *Alchemilla mollis*
- *Briza media*
- *Lavandula stoechas*
- *Melissa officinalis*
- *Miscanthus oligostachyus*
- *Nandina domestica*
- *Nigella damascena*
- *Papaver somniferum*
- *Pennisetum alopecuroides*
- *Phlomis fruticosa*
- *Phyllostachys nigra*
- *Physalis alkekengi*
- *Platycodon grandiflorus*
- *Senecio cineraria*
- *Stachys byzantina* "Big Ears"
- *Stipa tenuissima*
- *Trachelospermum jasminoides*

Lonicera periclymenum | *Papaver somniferum* | *Physalis alkekengi* | *Stachys byzantina* "Big Ears"

Water features

Water introduces movement, noise, and wildlife, and has a place in the family yard as long as you chooose an appropriate and safe (*see pp. 102–103*) water feature.

Waterfall The creation of a naturalistic stream and waterfall is a major undertaking requiring skill and knowledge, but it has an exciting and dynamic presence in the yard, and will be enjoyed by all family members.

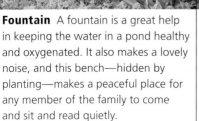

Timber decking A timber platform over a pond can be used as a dipping stage for examining the inhabitants. A net and container filled with pond water will reveal a hidden world. Children must be supervised when enjoying such an engrossing pastime.

Wildlife pond Every pond attracts wildlife, but you can make yours more appealing with a sloping bank by which frogs and other creatures can enter and leave. Frog spawn and some insect larvae are eaten by fish, so keep them in a separate pond.

Formal pond The stepping stones on this geometric pond dare you to walk across, so it would not be a suitable feature for families with young children. It could be enjoyed safely by supervised older children or teenagers, however, as would its modern design.

Fountain A fountain is a great help in keeping the water in a pond healthy and oxygenated. It also makes a lovely noise, and this bench—hidden by planting—makes a peaceful place for any member of the family to come and sit and read quietly.

Planting It is important to get the right mix of plants. Deep water aquatics, such as water lilies, help to shade the surface to prevent algal bloom. You should also include marginal plants at the edges of the pond and oxygenators in the depths.

Bubble pool If you have no space for a pond, or are worried about the safety implications for young children, you can still introduce water in the form of a bubble pool. Water trickles over this urn and collects in a tank underneath, then is pumped back up.

Pets in the backyard

It is not only family members who need to be able to enjoy the yard. Some pets spend a great deal of their time outdoors, and you can include features in your planning to help them enjoy it more too.

Chickens Chickens must be kept safe from foxes at night and love exploring the yard or a larger run during the day. They are woodland creatures and enjoy the shelter of a small tree or large shrub.

Dogs Dogs love to explore other yards, so provide strong, secure fencing to prevent them from escaping. Make sure any holes that appear in hedges or fences are quickly fixed or blocked up with chicken wire.

Goldfish Fish are a calming presence in the yard, but they must have a separate pond away from wildlife. In cold areas, they'll need a deep enough pond to avoid freezing in winter. A local nursery can advise on depths.

Guinea pigs Guinea pigs need a secure hutch and run, and will escape if let out into the yard. They enjoy eating many easily grown vegetables, so consider making a dedicated vegetable bed, filled with parsley and carrots.

Cats Cats crave a quiet, lofty position where they can bask in the sunshine. They love catnip, which can be easily grown in well-drained soil in full sun, and they eat grass to help their digestion.

Family friendly projects

Here are a number of manageable projects that will help you to create interest within your family's yard and gardens. There are quick, fun projects to spark children's interest, such as a cress head, a miniature wild animal garden, and a scarecrow, as well as features for wildlife—a bird food garland and a home for native bees. If you have more time and expertise, there are some larger projects, such as a useful and accessible raised bed, and a fragrant checkerboard of planting and paving that is fun for children to leap and jump around on, but attractive for adults too.

Growing sunflowers

Sunflowers are colorful giants and are one of the first flowers many children will recognize. A sunflower-growing competition appeals to any age of gardener.

Tip for success

As your sunflowers grow, tie the plants to bamboo canes to stop them from being blown over. Water them regularly and, for the best results, give the plants a regular feed.

1 Fill a 3½ in (9 cm) pot with seed compost. Biodegradable pots, such as those made from coir fibers, are particularly useful as they can be planted directly into the ground, but seedlings will do just as well when grown in plastic pots.

2 Plant one seed per pot, pushing it just below the surface. Sow in spring indoors or in a heated greenhouse. Seeds can also be planted directly into the ground in late spring and early summer, but for the largest plants, start early.

3 Once the seeds have germinated, keep the plants well watered. If you have started early, you may need to transplant into a larger pot while the plant is still indoors, in order to keep it growing strongly.

4 Pot your seedling into a larger pot or out into the ground when roots start showing through the bottom of the pot. When all danger of frost has passed, plant into ground that has been prepared with plenty of garden compost.

Alfalfa sprout heads

Sprouts germinate quickly. Growing from the top of this decorated pot, it looks like funny hair; a child-friendly combination of near-instant results and comedy.

Decorate several pots with different faces, using permanent markers, stick-on eyes, or even bits of wool stuck on with glue to make ears, mouths, and noses.

1 Once you have decorated your pot, make sure it has good drainage holes. If necessary, make your own with a drill or a sharp pair of scissors. Fill it with a multi-purpose compost, leaving around a 1¼ in (3 cm) gap at the top.

2 A piece of blotting paper will help to keep the seeds moist. Cut a circle just smaller than the top of the pot, place over the compost, and press it down firmly. Place the whole pot into a bowl of water to soak.

3 Once the paper is wet, lift the pot out and leave to drain. Measure out a small handful of alfalfa seeds and lightly scatter them over the surface. Don't sow too many as dense growth can lead to the stems rotting.

4 Put each container into a paper or plastic bag and leave in a bright, warm place, such as a windowsill. Check every day and remove as soon as the seeds have germinated. Water regularly and cut and eat when large enough.

Bird food garland

Wild birds are a lively and exciting feature of the yard and gardens. Tempt them into yours by creating an attractive garland of a variety of foods, to appeal to several different types of bird.

Tip for success

Bird cake is made with suet and so is quite slippery. After it has set, tie a knot at the bottom to stop it from slipping off. A small twig tied into the knot would make it really secure.

1 Pine cones make a useful base for bird food. A quick bird treat can be made by filling one with fat- and energy-rich peanut butter, a particularly good food in winter. Smear it over the pine cone, pushing it into all the gaps.

2 Choose a good-quality bird seed mix, as cheaper ones can occasionally be bulked up with split peas, dried rice or lentils (only good for larger species), or even dog biscuits. Make a pile on a flat surface.

3 Roll the peanut butter-covered cone in the seed mix, making sure there is no peanut butter left showing when you have finished. You can also press seed into the cone with your fingers to get a good amount in.

4 Suspend the cones from a length of raffia, string, or any other cord you have on hand, and hang it between branches of a tree or sturdy shrub, or between two upright posts of a pergola. Squirrels will probably enjoy this too!

Bird food garland *continued*

5 Bird food cakes are also easy to make. Slowly melt a pack of suet or lard in a saucepan and stir in some wild bird food mix. You can also add dried fruit, nuts, pinhead, oatmeal, or even cake.

6 Make a hole in the bottom of some empty yogurt (or similar) pots. Thread through a length of string and then fill each pot with the suet and bird seed mixture. Leave in a fridge until cool and set.

7 Gently ease the cake from the container. If it doesn't come out easily, stand the container in a bowl of warm water so that the suet melts slightly. Alternatively, you can let the birds eat the cake from the container.

8 For fruit and nut chains, thread a mixture of dried fruit and peanuts onto lengths of string using a needle with a large eye and a sharp point. Some peanuts contain a toxin that can kill birds, so buy from a reputable dealer.

9 Dried or fresh apple rings look attractive and are sought after by robins, thrushes, and wrens. Core and slice an apple, then tie together to create a chain. This is a good use for windfalls that have slightly gone over.

10 To put all of these bird treats together in a bird food garland, choose a spot with two sturdy branches with a gap between them and firmly attach a piece of raffia. Make sure it is not close to the ground.

11 Tie the treats to the raffia, then sit back and wait for the birds to discover them. At Christmas, this would make a festive decoration for a large conifer, giving the birds a bit of pampering at a tough time of year.

Planting an obelisk

An obelisk adds instant height and structure to a garden, and is particularly welcome in a garden planted mainly with low-growing perennials. It is a lovely way to display climbers.

Tip for success

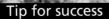

Many climbers need help to stay attached to their support. Use a soft garden twine and tie in a figure of eight to prevent the stem from rubbing against the structure.

1 Position your obelisk on an area of bare soil and push firmly into the ground. Placed on the corner of a bed, it will be prominent and dramatic, while further back, it will add solidity to the rest of the bed.

2 Dig a hole a short distance from the structure, larger than the plant's pot. Add compost to the base of the hole, then position the plant, leaning inward toward the obelisk. Backfill with soil, firm and water in well.

3 Spread the stems out and tie to the obelisk. This will need doing regularly as the plant grows. The general rule is to tie tightly around the support and loosely around the plant, to allow stems to expand and thicken.

4 To soften the impact of the new structure, plant around its base. You may want to mix a few bedding plants—for instant, summer-long color—with some perennials, which will flower and hide the obelisk base each year.

Making a scarecrow

A scarecrow is a lot of fun to make using old clothes and a bit of creativity. It is also a useful thing to have around, particularly in places where there aren't a lot of people.

Tip for success

When constructing your scarecrow's cross frame, use two nails, spaced slightly apart, to keep the horizontal piece firmly in place and prevent it from spinning around.

1 Create a cross frame from two lengths of wood. This will provide the basic shape of the body. Choose a postion near any particularly vulnerable crops and use a mallet to knock the vertical piece firmly into the ground.

2 You will need a selection of old clothes that you are happy to discard. Alternatively, look in thrift stores or garage sales for a suitable outfit. Feed the horizontal piece of wood through the shirt arms and secure.

3 Take a length of string or twine and tie it tightly around the bottom of the shirt to create a waist. This will also allow you to stuff the main part of the body without all of the stuffing falling out.

4 Just as with the waist, the sleeves of each shirt need tightly binding up to allow for successful stuffing. At a later stage, you could decide to sew or tie on a pair of stuffed gloves to give the scarecrow hands.

Making a scarecrow *continued*

5 Straw is the traditional stuffing material, and will give an authentically rustic look if bits are left sticking out. It is also environmentally friendly, should any escape. However, you could also use the innards from old pillows or quilts.

6 The pants will need to be stuffed before they are attached to the "body." Before starting to stuff, hold them up against the scarecrow first to see how long you should leave the legs, then tie string at that point.

7 Attach the pants by creating suspenders, tied through the belt loops on either side (or use real suspenders, of you have a pair). Make them secure by tying string through the back belt loop and around the frame.

8 Use an old pair of boots or shoes to finish off the body. If you are sure that you are not going to be using them again, make a hole in the back of the boot to allow you to tie them on to the base of the pants.

9 An old pillowcase stuffed with straw—pulled down over the top of the frame—makes a good base for a head as it can be molded into the right shape and creates a blank canvas on which to draw a face.

10 Once you have roughly the right shape, tie a piece of string around the base of the pillowcase, also wrapping it around the frame. Button the shirt up as high as necessary in order to hide this away.

11 No scarecrow is complete without straw hair, ideally sticking out from beneath an old hat. Secure across the center of the head using a needle and thread, and then flatten it down a little. You could also use wool.

12 Finally, some felt eyes, a nose, and a mouth will give the scarecrow a character of his own. Pens might run in the rain so instead use pipe cleaners, buttons, and old scraps of material; in fact, anything that can be sown into place.

Bee house

Solitary bees are excellent pollinators, but they can struggle to find suitable nesting sites. A homemade nesting box looks attractive and will encourage them into your garden and ensure you have bumper fruit crops every year.

Tip for success

Tie the raffia or string loosely around the base of the pot and then carefully push it upward, toward the rim. As the sides of the pot widen, so the hold tightens.

1 Use sharp pruners, loppers, or a hacksaw to cut short lengths of bamboo stalks. Don't worry about the thickness of the bamboo stalks; the natural variation in size will attract a range of different bee species.

2 Fill the base of a small terracotta pot with a thick layer of modeling clay and push the cut bamboo stalks into it. Continue until the pot is full and the stalks are sitting snugly inside the rim.

3 Stuff the gaps around the stalks with moss or dried grass to hold them firmly in place. Try to ensure that all stalks are pointing toward the ground, so that rainwater does not pour into the holes.

4 Tie a piece of raffia or gardening twine around the pot and use the excess twine to make a loop for hanging the pot from a hook. Or attach it to a wall in a sunny position sheltered from the wind, close to nectar-rich plants.

Patio plantings checkerboard

A checkerboard of pavers and planting is an attractive feature that can quickly turn into a children's play space; they won't be able to resist hopping across the patio.

1 Clear your chosen checkerboard area of all grass and weeds and then rake it over, making the area as flat and even as possible. At the same time, remove any stones you come across.

2 Use a wooden board—such as a scaffolding plank—to compact the soil, making it more even and easier to lay the pavers on to. Move it gradually across the area, walking across it each time it is laid.

3 Measure the pavers and then, on opposite sides of the area, mark out the measurements with sticks and stretch twine or string between them. Repeat on the other edges, making sure the lines are parallel and perpendicular.

4 The squares on which the pavers are going to be laid should be covered with sand to a depth of about 2 in (5 cm). This will give the pavers something to bed into, and will make laying and levelling much easier.

Patio plantings checkerboard *continued*

5 After you have put all of the sand in place it will need to be leveled out and consolidated. This is most easily done by "firming" it down lightly, all over the square, with the back of a rake.

6 Mix up a wet mortar of four parts sand (half and half sharp sand and building sand) to one part cement or use a ready mix. Place a trowel-full in each corner and one in the center. This will firmly hold the paver in place.

7 Put the paver carefully in its place and use the wooden end of a mallet gently to knock the corners until it is level. It is essential to use a small spirit level here, checking the level in all directions.

8 To bring the planted squares up to the level of the paved squares, fill in with topsoil. This will help with maintenance in the long run, particularly if you are sowing grass and will need to run a mower over the pavers.

9 Plant up your squares. We have used a creeping thyme, but other good choices would be *Soleirolia soleirolii*, chamomile "Treneague", or grass. Grass could be sown from seed in the fall or spring or cut pieces of turf to fit.

10 Water your plants in and then keep them well watered for the first season, until they are well established. Weed regularly until the plants knit together. New grass seed will need several months before it can be walked on.

11 Children are bound to create their own stories of stepping stones over swamps and fast-flowing rivers but they can also use colored (and temporary) chalk to make a game of hopscotch—and enjoy the scent when they miss a step.

Making a raised bed

A raised bed can be useful for several members of the family; filled with good topsoil they make perfect self-contained children's beds, and their height makes them easier to care for if you are in a wheelchair or have reduced mobility.

1 Dig out strips of turf wide enough to accommodate the timbers. Pressure-treated, softwood sleepers are an economical alternative to rot-resistant hardwoods like oak. You could also consider buying reclaimed hardwood.

2 Lay the timbers out in situ and check that they are level using a spirit level, or a plank of wood supporting a shorter spirit level. Check the levels diagonally between timbers, as well as along their length.

3 Ensure the base is square by checking that the diagonals are equal in length. For a perfect square or rectangular bed, it is a good idea to have the timbers pre-cut to size at a local lumber yard.

Making a raised bed *continued*

4 Using a rubber mallet, gently tap the wood so that it butts up against the adjacent piece; it should stand perfectly level and upright according to the readings on your spirit level. Remove soil as necessary.

5 Drill through the end timbers into the adjacent pieces at both the top and bottom to accommodate a couple of long, heavy-duty coach screws. Screw firmly into position, securing the base ready for the next level to be built.

6 Arrange the next set of timbers, making sure that these overlap the joints below to give the structure added strength. Check with a spirit level before screwing in the final set of fixings, as for step 5.

7 For the extra drainage required by plants, such as Mediterranean herbs and alpines, part fill the base with construction rubble or chippings. Then add sieved topsoil that is guaranteed free from perennial weeds.

How to make a mowing edge

1. Using a spare brick to measure the appropriate distance, set up a line of string to act as a guide. Dig out a strip of turf deep enough to accommodate the bricks plus 1 in (2.5 cm) of mortar.

2. Lay a level mortar mix in the bottom of the trench as a foundation for the bricks. Set them on top, leaving a small gap between each brick. Although this design is straight, mowing edges can also be fitted around curves.

3. With a spirit level, check that the bricks are aligned and slightly below the surface of the turf; use a rubber mallet to gently tap them into position. Once set in place, you will be able to mow straight over the bricks.

4. Finally, use a dry mix to mortar the joints between the bricks, working the mixture in with a trowel. Clean off the excess. The mowing edge makes maneuvering the mower easier, and minimizes the need to trim.

Spring bulbs

Bulbs are easy to plant and grow well in a pot. A planting of mixed spring bulbs will give quick, near-guaranteed results for kids and a colorful display that can be enjoyed by the rest of the family.

1 Choose a container with good drainage holes and then cover them with broken terracotta pots or tiles. They prevent the holes from getting clogged up with compost, which would stop water from draining away.

2 Some sun-loving bulbs, such as tulips, need really good drainage as they need to be kept fairly dry when dormant. They will not do well if sitting in moist soil. When planting these, add a layer of gravel to aid drainage further.

3 Fill the pot with compost (use bulb-planting or multi-purpose), to within 6 in (15 cm) of the rim. If using multi-purpose compost, improve its drainage by mixing in one part horticultural grit to every three parts of compost.

4 As a rule, bulbs should be planted at three times their own depth. Make sure the shoot (the pointed end) is facing upward. Then top up the pot with compost to within 2 in (5 cm) of the rim, to allow for easy watering.

Miniature landscape

Using small plants to make a miniature landscape fires the imagination and reduces the garden to a child's scale. Plastic farm or jungle animals, fairies, or dinosaurs bring the scene to life.

Tip for success

Gravel spread over the compost will help to conserve moisture in the summer. You might also choose to use it as a path meandering through your chosen landscape.

1   Choose a large, shallow tray, such as a seed tray. If there are no holes in the base, you will need to make some using a drill or sturdy pair of scissors. To aid drainage further, add course sand or gravel.

2   Fill the container with compost to about 1¼ in (3 cm) below the rim, carefully keeping the gravel evenly spread. Once it is full, position the major features, such as large pebbles and rocks or homemade fences and buildings.

3   Arrange your plants while still in containers, also deciding where best to position your animals. Think about other props you might want to use, such as rocks and pebbles. Give all the plants a good soak before planting.

4   Plant up your miniature garden. A good plant for linking your chosen small plants is the tiny-leaved *Soleirolia soleirolii* (mind-your-own-business), which makes an excellent "lawn."

Planting recipes

The following planting recipes will show you how to use plants in an imaginative and family friendly way, to interest and entertain children, parents, and grandparents. The symbols below are used in each recipe to indicate the conditions the plants prefer.

Key to plant symbols

♈ Plants given the RHS Award of Garden Merit

Soil preference

◌ Well-drained soil

◑ Moist soil

● Wet soil

Preference for sun or shade

☼ Full sun

☀ Partial or dappled shade

☀ Full shade

Hardiness ratings

❅❅❅ Fully hardy plants

❅❅ Plants that survive outside in mild regions or sheltered sites

❅ Plants that need protection from frost over winter

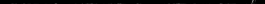

Pond in a pot

If you have a small yard, you may think that you have no space for a water feature, but there is no need to miss out on the aesthetic and wildlife benefits that a body of water can bring. A large pot or half barrel makes a great pond, and there are many smaller-scale pond plants that will fit in the container perfectly. It is true that larger-scale ponds are the easiest to maintain, as they are slower to warm up and cool down than smaller ponds, but you will be surprised by how much wildlife makes use of your little watery oasis.

Nymphaea "Pygmaea Helvola"
❄❄❄ ♦ ☀ ♆

Nymphaea "Pygmaea Rubra"
❄❄❄ ♦ ☀

Border basics

Size 24 in (60 cm) diameter
Suits The corner of a patio
Soil Aquatic compost
Site A spot that has sun for about half the day

Shopping list

- 1 x *Nymphaea* "Pygmaea Helvola"
- 1 x *Nymphaea* "Pygmaea Rubra"
- 1 x *Typha minima*
- 1 x *Myriophyllum aquaticum*

Planting and aftercare

Half barrels, when soaked, should become watertight, but it is hard to get them wet enough and you may find it easier to use a piece of pond liner that is stapled or tacked around the insides of the pot. Once you have done this, fill with water. Ideally, this should be rainwater, but use tap water if you don't have a water barrel. Put all the plants into aquatic planting baskets—special plastic mesh containers filled with aquatic compost. Place a layer of pea gravel or similar over the surface of each pot and then put on the bottom of the container. Many oxygenating plants do not need planting and simply float just above or below the surface. A pile of stones or a small wooden ramp will allow wildlife to find its way in and out.

Typha minima
❄❄❄ ♦ ☀

Myriophyllum aquaticum
❄❄❄ ♦ ☀

Alternative plant idea

Nymphaea "Froebelii"
❄❄❄ ♦ ☀

Herb border

A herb garden is a feature the whole family can enjoy. Children will enjoy the tastes, smells, and textural qualities of many of these plants; parents and grandparents can enjoy cooking with them or even just looking at them as they are as pretty as they are useful. They rub along very nicely in an ornamental vegetable patch with other edibles such as purple cabbages and frilly leaved lettuces. Many herbs are at their best in a sunny position, but chives and parsley can both be grown successfully in more shady positions, if necessary.

Border basics

Size 10x5 ft (3x1.5 m)
Suits A border in a vegetable garden or kitchen garden
Soil Well-drained
Site Sunny

Shopping list

- 1 x *Foeniculum vulgare* "Purpureum"
- 1 x *Salvia officinalis* "Purpurascens"
- 1 x *Rosmarinus officinalis*
- 5 x *Petroselinum crispum*
- 10 x *Allium schoenoprasum*

Planting and aftercare

Silver-leaved Mediterranean herbs, such as sage and rosemary, really need a well-drained soil. If yours has less than perfect drainage, dig in plenty of horticultural grit before starting to plant. Do not simply put grit into the bottom of planting holes, as this creates a sump that water will run into during heavy downpours. Rosemary and sage are evergreen and relatively large, so use them to anchor the rest of the planting. Fennel has a transparent, wispy growth, so can look good near the front of the border. Chives make excellent edging plants. The parsley will need to be grown from seed each year, but all other plants are evergreen or perennial and will just require feeding and mulching each year.

Foeniculum vulgare "Purpureum"
❋❋❋ ◊◊ ☼

Salvia officinalis "Purpurascens"
❋❋ ◊◊ ☼ ☼ ♆

Rosmarinus officinalis
❋❋ ◊ ☼

Petroselinum crispum
❋❋❋ ◊◊ ☼ ☼

Allium schoenoprasum
❋❋❋ ◊ ☼ ☼

Alternative plant idea

Borago officinalis
❋❋❋ ◊ ☼ ☼

Butterfly paradise

If you have a sunny, sheltered border, you have the makings of a butterfly garden. Butterflies need to be able to bask in sunshine, and their delicate wings cannot cope with very much wind. They are attracted to simple, single flowers that are rich in nectar. This vibrantly colored border reaches its peak in late summer, but to really support the butterflies, try to plant other plants nearby that will provide nectar throughout the year. The addition of a butterfly feeding station and hibernation house would almost guarantee an impressive show.

Border basics

Size 10x10 ft (3x3 m)
Suits A border
Soil Moisture-retentive but well-drained
Site Sheltered, in full sun

Shopping list

- 3 x *Aster amellus* "King George"
- 3 x *Rudbeckia fulgida* var. *deamii*
- 3 x Sedum
- 3 x *Solidago* "Golden Wings"

Planting and aftercare

Clear the ground of weeds and prepare the soil by digging in plenty of organic matter, such as garden compost, composted bark chips, or mushroom compost. Position the plants on the ground, while still in their pots. Keep them in clumps of three or in drifts. Try several positions until they look right. It is traditional to put larger plants, such as solidago, toward the back of a border, and smaller plants, such as sedum, toward the front, to create a bank of color. However, lovely effects can be created by using tall but translucent plants such as *Verbena bonariensis*, toward the front of a border. After planting, keep plants well watered for the first few months, while the roots get well established.

Aster amellus "King George"
❀❀❀ ◊◌ ☼ ☀ ♉

Rudbeckia fulgida var. *deamii*
❀❀❀ ◊◌ ☼ ☀ ♉

…lum
❋ ❋ ◌ ☼

Solidago "Goldenrod"
❋ ❋ ❋ ◌ ☼

Echinacea purpurea
❋ ❋ ❋ ◌ ☼

Alternative plant idea

The giant garden

Large plants that dwarf little people can be a wonderful addition to a children's garden. Oversized plants do not require huge gardens, and this bold planting scheme can actually make a small garden look bigger than one planted up with lots of small ones. Gunnera is the biggest and most impressive of these and should be given center stage, the other plants complementing it, some in the ground, some in pots. The gunnera will need a lot of moisture at the roots, and should be planted in bog garden conditions for the biggest leaves.

Border basics

Size 12x6 ft (4x2 m)
Suits A hidden corner at the end of a garden
Soil Moisture retentive but well-drained
Site Shady

Shopping list

- 1 x *Cordyline australis* "Red Star"
- 1 x *Cordyline australis* "Variegata"
- 1 x *Fatsia japonica*
- 1 x *Gunnera manicata*
- 3 x *Astilbe* x *arendsii*

Sowing and aftercare

Gunnera and astilbe will both grow in normal conditions, but they will do better in a bog garden. To create a small bog garden, dig out an area to a depth of about 24 in (60 cm) and line with a pond liner. Pierce this several times and then backfill with the excavated soil. This area will naturally stay moister than the surrounding soil, but the plants will benefit from being watered during dry periods. The fatsia and cordylines will grow well in normal soil, but it is a good idea to improve the soil with organic matter before planting. Red-leaved cordylines are less hardy than the colored-leaved species, so in cold areas, wrap the stem and crown with burlap or tarps over winter.

Gunnera manicata
❄❄❄ ◐ ◖ ☀ ◐ ▽

Cordyline australis "Red Star"
❄❄ ◌ ☀ ◐

Astilbe x *arendsii*
❄❄❄ ◐ ◖ ☀

Fatsia japonica
❄❄❄ ◐ ☀

Cordyline australis "Variegata"
❄❄ ◌ ☀ ◐

Alternative plant idea

Catalpa bignonioides
❄❄❄ ◌ ◐ ☀

Tropical paradise

A tropical border is one of the most exciting plantings, filled with bold, colorful plants and reminiscent of a child's fantasy jungle. However, this is also high-maintenance gardening because many of the plants used are tender or not entirely hardy, and so need some winter protection. This is easier if you have a frost-free greenhouse or shed that you can move plants to in winter. If you have the equipment, and think you are up to the challenge, there is little to rival a tropical border in late summer.

Border basics

Size 10x6 ft (3x2 m)
Suits A deep border
Soil Well-drained but enriched with organic matter
Site Sunny

Shopping list

- 1 x *Musa ornata*
- 3 x *Canna* "Durban"
- 1 x *Verbena bonariensis*
- 3 x *Dahlia* "Grenadier"

Sowing and aftercare

As some of the plants in a tropical border are tender, it is important to wait until late spring, when all danger of frost has passed, to plant out. *Verbena bonariensis* is half-hardy and can stay in the soil all year in some zones, but all of the other plants will need some help to get through winter. Cannas can sometimes cope with winter frosts if given a thick mulch after they have died down, but it is safer to lift the whole plant and store it in a frost-free place. Likewise, the tubers of *Dahlia* "Grenadier" will need lifting, but if you choose a hardier dahlia, such as "Bishop of Llandaff," you will save yourself this trouble. Most musas are not hardy and will need to be taken indoors, but plant *Musa basjoo* and you can get away with just wrapping the stems in winter.

Musa ornata
❄◊☀♛

Canna "Durban"
❄❄◊☀

Verbena bonariensis
❄❄◊◊☀♛

Dahlia "Grenadier"
❄◊☀♛

Alternative plant idea

Dahlia "Bishop of Llandaff"
❄❄◊◊☀♛

Heaven scent

Scent is an essential part of the yard and gardens, and an area filled with scented plants will always be well loved. The scented elements of this border are roses and lavender. Such plants look wonderful in a cottage garden with plants such as sisyrinchium and hardy geranium, all in soft pastel shades.

A narrow path between two large, overflowing borders brings visitors close enough to smell the plants, and forces them to brush against the fragrant stems of the lavender as they pass by, releasing its scent.

Border basics

Size 2 borders, each 10x6 ft (3x2 m)
Suits Borders either side of a narrow path
Soil Well-drained but fertile
Site Full sun

Shopping list per border

- 1 x *Rosa* "Felicia"
- 3 x *Geranium pratense*
- 3 x *Sisyrinchium striatum*
- 5 x *Lavandula angustifolia* "Hidcote"

Planting and aftercare

Lavender likes well-drained soil, so you may need to add plenty of horticultural sand to the beds before you start, concentrating on the area on either side of the path, where the lavender hedge will be planted. Plant the lavender in a straight line on either side of the path with a spacing of about 20 in (50 cm) between each one of the plants.

Roses, on the other hand, like a rich, fertile soil, but they will not mind the extra drainage given by the sand too much. It is a good idea, though, to dig out a deep planting hole for the rose and fill it with organic matter (such as garden compost or composted bark) mixed with soil. This will ensure that the soil stays moist—but continue to water for at least the first season.

Rosa "Felicia"
❋❋❋ ◊ ☼ ♛

Geranium pratense
❋❋❋ ◊◑ ☼ ◐ ☀

Sisyrinchium striatum
❋❋❋ ◊ ☼

Lavandula angustifolia "Hidcote"
❋❋❋ ◊ ☼ ♛

Alternative plant idea

Rosa Pink Bells
❋❋❋ ◊ ☼

Meadow planting

Meadows are magical places for children to play, losing themselves among the tall grasses and brightly colored flowers. However, a meadow is a hard thing to maintain in a small yard. Although a planting of cornflower annuals looks wonderful at the height of summer, there are long periods when it is not flowering, or is past its best. Therefore, this is a project that most suits larger yards, where garden space is not so precious.

Border basics

Size As large as possible
Suits The end of a large yard, or areas left to scrappy lawn
Soil Poor, freely draining soil that has not been enriched by fertilizer
Site Open and sunny

Shopping list

Cornflower seed mix, containing:
- *Leucanthemum vulgare*
- *Papaver rhoeas*
- *Agrostemma githago*
- *Centaurea cyanus*
- *Chrysanthemum segetum*
- *Anthemis arvensis*

Planting and aftercare

Before sowing a wildflower meadow, it is essential that the ground is cleared of weeds and grasses. Any left in the ground will outcompete the wild flowers. An effective way of doing this is to use a glyphosate-based weedkiller, but many people will find this contrary to the spirit of wildflower meadow creation. Instead, removing the topsoil removes weeds and reduces the fertility of the ground, helping wild flowers to compete.

Once the ground is clear, broadcast sow the seed in the fall or spring. Leave uncut until flowering is over and seed set. Trim or scythe the growth, then leave it to dry where it falls for a few days so that seeds have a chance to fall to the ground.

Leucanthemum vulgare
❄❄❄ ◊ ◖ ☼ ☀

Papaver rhoeas
❄❄❄ ◊ ☼

Agrostemma githago
❄❄❄ ◊ ☼

Centaurea cyanus
❄❄❄ ◊ ☼

Chrysanthemum segetum
❄❄❄ ◊ ☼

Alternative plant idea

Anthemis punctata
❄❄ ◊ ☼

Snack garden

Children get a thrill from picking and eating their favorite foods right off the plant. The idea of a snack garden is to gather together food plants that appeal to children, particularly those that can be eaten without cooking. In addition to the strawberries and tomatoes shown here, you could include carrots (sown close together to be pulled up and eaten young and sweet), sugarsnap peas and radishes. This garden also serves a great educational purpose: they will never think that tomatoes only come from supermarkets.

Border basics

Size 6x3 ft (2x1 m)
Suits A raised bed or the corner of a courtyard
Soil Fertile, well-drained
Site Sunny, possibly with a little shade

Shopping list

- 1 x strawberry
- 1 x wild strawberry
- 1 x tomato plant
- 1 x mint
- 1 x parsley
- 1 x chives

Planting and aftercare

A dedicated raised bed would be perfect for a snack garden, but it could equally be a collection of containers, gathered together in one area of a garden. If planting in containers, you will need to make sure you provide adequate drainage by putting broken pots over the drainage holes. The herbs, strawberries, and wild strawberries are hardy and can be planted in the ground and left there year round, but tomatoes will need to be sown from seed in spring indoors and then planted out once all danger of frost has passed. Choose a cherry tomato such as "Gardener's Delight" or "Sungold" for their sweet taste, early ripening, and size.

Strawberry
❄❄❄ ◌ ☼

Wild strawberry
❄❄❄ ◌ ☼

Tomatoes
❄◌ ◖ ☼

Mentha spicata (mint)
❄❄❄ ◖ ◌ ☼

Petroselinum crispum (parsley)
❄❄❄ ◌ ◖ ☼ ◑

Allium schoenoprasum (chives)
❄❄❄ ◌ ☼ ◑

Wildlife garden

Attracting wildife into the yard brings it to life, and a pond is a magnet for wildlife. The planting in and around it helps to shade and oxygenate the water to keep it healthy, so allowing the creatures that use it to thrive. It also provides cover and shelter. You don't have to stick to traditional pond plants in order to create an attractive and wildlife-friendly planting. As the planting moves into drier ground further from the pond, plant colorful and long-flowering perennials, such as hardy geraniums, to provide interest and season-long nectar.

Border basics

Size 12x9 ft (4x3 m)
Suits The margins and surrounds of a pond
Soil Moist
Site Full sun or partial shade

Shopping list

- 1 x *Caltha palustris*
- 5 x *Cirsium rivulare* "Atropurpureum"
- 3 x *Hemerocallis lilioasphodelus*
- 3 x *Iris sibirica*
- 5 x *Iris ensata*
- 3 x *Geranium* "Brookside"

Planting and aftercare

Margin plants such as *Caltha palustris* should be planted onto a shallow shelf on the edge of the pond, as they like to be completely immersed in water, but not planted too deep. They should be planted first into a planting basket filled with aquatic compost. Cover this with pea gravel to prevent the compost from floating away.

Moisture-loving plants, such as cirsium, hemerocallis, and iris, will do best in moist soil, so if the soil around the pond is not naturally damp, create a bog garden by digging out an area and lining it with pond liner, perforated with a garden fork. Refill the liner with soil and then plant it up.

Caltha palustris
❄❄❄ ● ☼ ♔

Cirsium rivulare "Atropurpureum"
❄❄❄ ◌◌ ☼

Hemerocallis lilioasphodelus
❄❄❄ ◌◌● ☼ ♔

Iris sibirica
❄❄❄ ◌● ☼ ♔

Iris ensata
❄❄❄ ◌ ☼ ◑ ♔

Geranium "Brookside"
❄❄❄ ◌◌● ☼ ◑ ♔

Strawberry tower

Alpine strawberries are a dainty but flavor-packed version of the fruits we all know and love. They are even better suited to pot culture than normal strawberries, as they are so dimunutive in size. Unlike normal strawberries, which must be grown in the full sun for the best tasting berries, these woodland plants will grow and crop quite happily in some dappled shade. A strawberry planter or tower is a tall pot with side pockets for planting. It won't provide enough of a crop for making jam, but there should be enough for scattering over your breakfast cereal for a few weeks in the summer. Add a couple of shade-tolerant annuals, such as these begonias, for aesthetic appeal.

Border basics

Size Large strawberry pot
Suits Patio or courtyard
Soil Potting soil
Site Light shade

Shopping list

- 5 x Alpine strawberry
- 1 x Angel wings begonia
- 3 x *Begonia* Cocktail Series

Planting and aftercare

Line the base of the tower with broken terracotta or stones to cover the drainage holes, then start to fill with soil. When you reach the level of the lowest pockets, position the strawberries or other chosen plants in them and feed in compost around the rootballs. Carry on filling the tower in the same way until all the pockets and the top are planted. Keep the plants well watered during the summer; they must not be allowed to dry out while the fruits are swelling and ripening. Feed with a tomato fertilizer during spring and summer. Continue to pick the fruits to encourage the plants to carry on producing. Also deadhead the flowering plants to maintain their display.

Alpine strawberry flower
❄❄ ◊ ◊ ☀

Angel wings begonia
❄◊ ◊ ☀

Alpine strawberry in fruit
❄❄ ◊ ◊ ☀

Begonia Cocktail Series
❄◊ ◊ ☀

Companion planting

The practice of companion planting harnesses the different properties of plants to create a plant community. It is a traditional technique much used by organic growers to create better growing conditions. It works as well in a patio container as it does on a community plot. French marigolds are a classic companion plant, as they are attractive to hoverflies, which feast on aphids. They also emit a pungent odor, which helps to repel pests. Scent is an important element of companion planting, and using strongly smelling culinary herbs, such as thyme, can confuse pests as to the location of their prey.

Ocimum basilicum (basil)
❄ ◌ ◐ ☀

Tagetes French group
❄ ◌ ☀

Border basics

Size Containers of any size
Suits A patio
Soil Organic multi-purpose compost
Site Sunny and fairly sheltered

Shopping list

- 1 x basil
- 2 x *Tagetes* French group
- 1 x cherry tomato such as "Gardener's Delight"
- 2 x variegated thyme

Planting and aftercare

Make sure the base of the container has adequate drainage holes and then cover these with broken pots to ensure the holes do not get blocked with compost. Fill the container about two-thirds full, and then plant. Place the tomato toward the back of the container, the medium-sized basil in the center, and the two thymes next to the edge, where they will trail, softening the effect. As this is quite a densely planted pot, it needs watering to make sure it doesn't dry out. It will also need a weekly feed with a high potassium tomato fertilizer, as soon as the first truss of flowers have started to turn into fruits. Tie the tomato on to a stake for support.

Tomato
❄❄❄ ◐ ☀

Thymus serpyllum 'Variegatus' (thyme)
❄❄❄ ◐ ☀

Alternative plant idea

Viola tricolor
❄❄❄ ◌ ◐ ☀ ◑

Taking care of your family

This section addresses some of the major concerns and hazards that can be created when planning your family's yard and gardens. Older and frailer members of the family will need to have easy access to the yard if they are going to enjoy it in its entirety. For young children, it is important to know which plants are poisonous and to consider the safety of gardening chemicals and water features. Pets can cause problems in your yard and gardens, but there are solutions. Finally, this section covers storage ideas that will allow tools and toys to be hidden away at the end of the day.

Access

Make your yard easier to access and move around in as you get older, and you will be able to enjoy gardening it for a lot longer.

Well lit steps While steps are a hazard to the elderly and disabled, sometimes they cannot be avoided in the yard. Where there are changes of level, a set of stairs is often preferable to a slope. Make sure yours are well built, with no loose bricks and—perhaps more importantly—well lit at night. Here, small lights have been set into the risers. This is an excellent solution, as you will not cast shade over the steps as you walk up them.

Wide and level paths A wide, level path provides the perfect way for a wheelchair user to move unhindered around the yard. Wide paths that allow two people to easily walk side by side are also helpful if you are unsteady on your feet, as they allow someone to walk with you, or for the easy use of a walking stick or other support. Such wide paths may be made primarily for the elderly or infirm, but they are also useful for toddlers, who are easily and painfully undone by loose bricks, and who greatly appreciate a hard, smooth surface on which to ride tricycles and other play vehicles.

The quality of your hard landscaping becomes more important as you become less physically able. Loose bricks cause a tripping hazard, so have all your hard landscaping done by a qualified professional with references.

Level seating on slopes Steeply sloping back yards can be among the most attractive, but they have major drawbacks, particularly if you are elderly or disabled. It can become impossible even to reach the far end of a sloping yard. One of the simplest ways you can make such a yard more accessible is to install level seating at points along the path. These provide a natural resting place where visitors and gardeners can stop and catch their breath, and will mean that the far reaches of the yard open up to them.

Terracing a slope is a major job, involving earth moving and the building of retaining walls, but it is often well worth the effort where the slope is extreme. It makes the space easier for everyone to use, turning an annoying slope into a beautiful, well-used, and relatively accessible yard.

Hard edging to raised beds Raised beds can have a double purpose in the accessible yard. They are excellent for bringing the plants and soil up a level, but they can also act as perching points from which to work, or just take a rest.

Railroad sleepers make good, wide beds. Here, they have been laid on their edges, which creates height with just a few sleepers. However, when they are stacked one on top of the other, they make a sturdy, wide wall, which can easily be sat on and worked from. It does take quite a few sleepers to achieve any worthwhile height, so it will be more expensive to build, in which case you might want to consider creating a wide-topped raised bed from bricks.

If the raised bed is adjacent to a lawn, make maintenance easier by laying a mowing strip of bricks.

Stepping stones Bare ground can get muddy in the spring and fall, making parts of the yard inaccessible to everyone, except, perhaps, the rubber boot-wearing toddler. Stepping stones are a good way of keeping pathways open whatever the weather. Here, a leafy woodland path of bark chippings has log rounds set into it, which perfectly blend into the setting. Most often, stepping stones are made from stone or concrete pavers, set into the ground, and these can be safer in winter, since they are less likely to become slippery. Chicken wire stretched over wood stepping stones and firmly nailed in place can help prevent accidents from happening.

Stepping stones can be just as useful across a lawn, where you do not want a full path but need to have all-weather access. Set along the course of a washing line they allow you to hang out washing even when the ground is wet.

Handrails Wherever there is a falling hazard in your yard, be sure to install a handrail. This pretty bridge and stream would be a major safety headache without such a sturdy handrail. It has been made so that its chunky proportions allow children to dawdle and lean against it, and enjoy playing safely beside the water.

Handrails can also be useful for helping young children and the elderly to steady themselves when walking up slopes and flights of steps. So consider installing them wherever any members of the family might struggle or trip. A handrail for children will need to be set lower than one for adults, but you can buy versions with rails at two levels, as pictured here.

Safety

Safety is important for everyone, but will be a high priority where young children use the yard. They are naturally inquisitive and prone to accidents, and so it is important to be aware of any major hazards that may come their way.

Learning about safety

A few accidents are inevitable, and if they happen in the relative safety of the family yard, can be a valuable learning experience. There is a move against covering the ground with unnaturally soft play surfaces, as this gives children the impression that they can fall with impunity. Likewise, they will soon learn which plants to avoid after a few pricked fingers and if you show them what is and isn't safe. A few knocks in the yard will help prepare children for the outside world, although there are, of course, some back yard accidents that are particularly nasty and are best avoided. Take precautions against these, and then relax about the minor scrapes.

Lock pesticides away In a child's hands, pesticides and other gardening chemicals can be extremely dangerous. Always keep chemicals in an inaccessible, padlocked cupboard and take care to dispose of them properly.

Clean algae from paving Algae can cause a slipping hazard for all members of the family, regardless of age. So, in shady, damp areas, pressure wash regularly to remove slippery moss and algae.

Protective clothing Putting on gloves when gardening will prevent you from getting hurt by thorns or sharp tools. Steel toe-capped boots guard against foot injuries when digging or moving large plants or pots around.

Wasp traps Wasps have a particularly unpleasant sting, so make a wasp trap from a jar filled with a sugary liquid and with a small hole in the top. Wasps are drawn into such traps, but cannot escape, and drown.

Stake toppers Supporting stakes can be a hazard for the gardener in the family, who will be the one most likely to poke his or her eye while bending over borders. Colored stake toppers make them more visible.

Pond cover Many parents fill in ponds because of the danger they present. Pond covers, however, make them safe. Strong grids for placing over the top of ponds (or just below the surface) can be bought cut to size.

Thorns and sharp leaves Pampas grass does not look hazardous, but it has razor-sharp leaves. Many plants have thorns or sharp points, so if you love it, plant it anyway, but teach children of the danger.

Pets

Pets are members of the family, too, and can be a delightful presence in the yard. However, they can also make a nuisance of themselves. Each animal brings its own set of problems and concerns you will need to address.

Fence dogs in Dogs love being in the yard, but really need more extensive space to run arond in than most of us can provide. Provide strong boundaries and expect a few escape attempts, and exercise yours regularly in a park or other large open space.

Collars on cats Unfortunately, many otherwise lovable cats love hunting down small birds and mammals. A collar fitted with a bell or ultrasonic warning device can give wildlife a head start. Also consider keeping your cat indoors at dawn and dusk, when birds are most active.

Confine small animals Rabbits will eat almost any plant in your gardens, so either keep them in their own run all of the time, or protect your plants. Locked night-time hutches are essential to keep rabbits and guinea pigs safe from predators such as foxes.

Separate area for chickens Chickens are great characters in the yard and help to keep down pests, such as slugs and snails, but they can wreak havoc with borders, scratching up all of the young growth as it emerges. Protect plants or keep the chickens in a run.

Common problems with dogs in yards

Dogs and lawns in particular are not a great mix. Larger dogs can cause big problems, turning lawns to mud in fall and spring; and all sizes of dog cover lawns with yellowing circles of dying grass in the summer. In fact, you may find it easier to give up on your lawn altogether and opt for a gravel surface instead.

Dead, yellow circles will form unless you can water immediately after.

Dogs love to dig, so protect any precious plants from their attentions.

Try to prevent your dog from disturbing neighbors in their yards.

Precautionary measures

There are a few measures you can take that will allow your animals to enjoy the yard relatively unimpeded and without wrecking all of your hard work. You should also take measures to keep pets and wild animals apart, which means that the local wildlife can also have the benefit of using your yard and gardens without fear of interruption.

Use chicken wire Chicken wire, strung between stakes around your borders will keep chickens out. Bury some of the wire under the ground to stop rabbits from digging in.

Dense planting Cats like to do their business on bare earth, so try to develop a dense layer of ground-covering plants on your borders, and they will go elsewhere.

Site bird feeders in the open Birds need to be able to see that there are no predators lurking nearby, so site feeders in the open near to a dense shrub for them to escape into.

Plants to avoid

Most plants are harmless, but there are a few you may want to avoid. Some cause hayfever, some irritate the skin, and others are poisonous if eaten.

Allergies Hayfever is caused by an allergy to pollen, and when you get it depends on which pollen you are allergic to. Wind-pollinated plants, with fine, air-borne pollen cause the problem. In spring, the main source of pollen is from trees, and through summer, lawn grasses are the worst culprits. You can make a garden that is filled only with insect-pollinated plants (*see pp.138–139*), but pollen is in the air, so you are unlikely to be able to avoid the problem altogether.

Hazel It is the beautiful long hazel catkins rather than the rest of the tree that cause the hayfever problems. The pollen they dispense is extremely fine and carried on the wind to pollinate other hazels in the area.

Hawthorn This shrub is one of the few insect-pollinated plants that cause hayfever. An allergy to its pollen is fairly rare, but it tends to cause quite a strong hayfever reaction in its sufferers.

Common skin irritants

Euphorbia schillingii All euphorbias are bad skin irritants. They are particularly so when cut, as the problem is with the milky sap that is exuded from the cuts. Irritation is worse on warm, sunny days.

Echium vulgare The stems of echium are covered in short, rough hairs that can cause irritation and itching on contact with skin. Wear gloves when handling young plants or cutting down old flower spikes.

Ruta graveolens Herb of Grace (or rue) is a severe skin irritant, especially if you are working on it in sunlight. Chemicals released from within the leaves react to the sun and cause irritation, itching, and blistering.

Common poisonous plants

Aconitum All parts of this imposing perennial plant are toxic to humans if accidentally eaten, and poison can even be absorbed through the skin.

Calla palustris If eaten, the bog arum *Calla palustris* can cause severe irritation and swelling to the mouth and throat. Severe skin irritant, too.

Colchicum autumnale "Pleniflorum' Both the flowers and the leaves of this pretty fall-flowering bulb are poisonous.

Digitalis Eating any part of a foxglove can cause severe poisoning, which is likely to be fatal, but poisoning is rare as it tastes so terrible.

Ipomoea purpurea The seeds of this plant contain powerful halucinogens, but they are only released if the seeds are crushed and then swallowed.

Laburnum The seeds and seed pods of laburnum are very attractive to children, but all parts are poisonous. Pets may also be poisoned by it.

Nerium oleander All parts of this plant are extremely poisonous, but the plant has an unpalatable, bitter taste, and so poisoning is rare.

Ricinus communis "Carmencita" All parts are poisonous, but the poison ricin is in the seed coat. There are very few cases of poisoning though.

Taxus baccata "Fastigiata" The poisonous seed surrounded by red flesh is attractive to children. Leaves are also poisonous.

Storage

So many family back yards are strewn with plastic toys. If this isn't for you, imaginative storage is the key to keeping the yard neat and clear and prevent it from becoming a dumping ground for toys, tools, and garbage cans.

Dealing with back yard clutter

The more the family grows, the more things you acquire, and many of them end up in the yard. Find ways to put toys away near where they are used, rather than having to move everything into the garage or shed at the end of the day. Buckets and shovels can live under the sandbox lid; bikes and tricycles can be chained to a bike rack in the front yard if you don't have a garage; toys can be secreted away beneath seating.

A regular clear-out will help keep the yard free of unused toys. A garage sale can be fun for everyone and raise a bit of cash, even if it does end up being spent on new toys.

Back yard shed   A shed provides a large amount of storage space but will quickly be filled. Consider putting other storage—shelves, stacking boxes, and hangers—within it to keep it neat and to maximize the space.

Tool rack   A simple rack such as this one, made from a piece of wood attached to the wall with nails driven into it, will keep all of your tools both neat and tidy and successfully out of the way.

Lift-up lids on seating   Seats that double as storage are an ingenious way of making the most of a small yard. At the end of the day, simply throw all the toys inside to reclaim the space.

Simple shelving Shelving in the shed or out in the yard will always be put to good use. These terracotta pots are being kept neat and they make an attractive display at the same time.

Lids on sandboxes Sandboxes should always have well-fitting lids. Cats will use sandboxes as cat litter trays, given the chance, and contact with cat feces is a source of toxoplasmosis, which can damage the brain or eyes.

Recycling bins Garbage cans and recycling bins can take up a large amount of space in the house, garage, or yard. This shelved container, with its quirky green roof, keeps them neatly hidden away.

Composters and water barrels Composters aren't very attractive, but they can be hidden behind a small hedge. Water barrels can be similarly disguised, or you can buy slimline ones that fit snugly against walls and into corners.

Plant guide

A family yard should be filled with garden plants. This plant guide has been arranged in useful sections so that you can easily choose plants that will suit your family's needs. The symbols below indicate the conditions the plants prefer.

Key to plant symbols

♔   **Plants given the RHS Award of Garden Merit**

Soil preference

○   **Well-drained soil**

◐   **Moist soil**

●   **Wet soil**

Preference for sun or shade

☼   **Full sun**

◐   **Partial or dappled shade**

✷   **Full shade**

Hardiness ratings

✳✳✳   **Fully hardy plants**

✳✳   **Plants that survive outside in mild regions or sheltered sites**

✳   **Plants that need protection from frost over winter**

Low-maintenance plants

Anemone hupehensis var. japonica
Japanese anemones produce copious flowers just as other perennials are fading away. Once established, these undemanding fall stalwarts will bring height to the border and flower over a long period in shades of white, pink, and purple.

H: 24–36 in (60–90 cm); **S**: 16 in (40 cm) ❄❄❄ ◊ ☼ ☼

Euonymus fortunei "Emerald 'n' Gold"
This evergreen shrub makes a bright, year-round ground cover for awkward spots. It is equally happy against a wall, where it will slowly climb and form a lovely variegated backdrop for other plants.

H: 24 in (60 cm); **S**: 36 in (90 cm) ❄❄❄ ◊ ☼ ☼ ♈

Fuchsia "Mrs. Popple"
Once established, hardy fuchsias such as "Mrs. Popple" flower from early summer up until the first frosts. "Mrs. Popple" is the classic cerise and purple coloring, but there are many others, some even more blowsy, but others slender and sophisticated.

H: 3 ft (1 m); **S**: 3 ft (1 m) ❄❄❄ ◊ ◊ ☼ ☼ ♈

Geranium himalayense "Gravetye"
Hardy geraniums make wonderfully colorful ground cover plants, and are smothered in flower all summer long. They require little attention. Some of them are fairly rampant, and you will have to lift and divide after a few years.

H: 12 in (30 cm); **S**: 24 in (60 cm) ❄❄❄ ◊ ☼ ☼ ♈

Hydrangea arborescens "Annabelle"
If you want flowers in a shady spot, go for a hydrangea. Those of "Annabelle" are among the loveliest. The plant produces huge white balls of flowers, complemented by an array of smaller green ones. Prune in spring to stop the plant getting too leggy.

H: 8 ft (2.5 m); **S**: 8 ft (2.5 m) ❄❄❄ ◊ ◊ ☼ ☼ ♈

Ophiopogon planiscapus "Nigrescens"
This ground cover plant has the darkest leaves you will find, which makes it useful to contrast against more colorful plants. Patches increase slowly over several years. The leaves still look good in winter.

H: 8 in (20 cm); **S**: 12 in (30 cm) ❄❄❄ ◊ ◊ ☼ ☼ ♈

Phormium **"Sundowner"**
The leaves of "Sundowner" contain streaks of pink, yellow, olive green, and copper. It is evergreen and slowly grows into an impressive clump. Grow it as a back-of-the-border plant as a foil for summer plants, then let it come into its own in the winter.

H: 6 ft (2 m); **S**: 6 ft (2 m)
❄❄ ◊ ◔ ☼ ♈

Picea glauca **var.** *albertiana* **"Conica"**
They may be low maintenance, but most dwarf conifers are very dull. However, *Picea glauca* var. *albertiana* "Conica" looks more like a piece of topiary than a typical dwarf conifer, its tiny, dense leaves forming a conical shape without trimming.

H: 6–20 ft (2–6 m); **S**: 3–8 ft (1–2.5 m) ❄❄❄ ◊ ◔ ☼

Pittosporum **"Garnettii"**
The gray-green and cream coloring of *Pittosporum* "Garnetti"'s small, wavy leaves makes it a particularly fine foil for flowering plants such as roses. The stems are delicate and almost black, and the whole plant has a refined air about it.

H: 10–15 ft (3–5 m); **S**: 6–12 ft (2–4 m) ❄◊ ◔ ☼ ☼ ♈

Pulmonaria officinalis **Cambridge Blue Group**
Pulmonarias are excellent additions to the spring garden, bringing color when all else is dull. They are healthy herbaceous perennials that come back reliably year after year and also seed themselves around the garden.

H: 12 in (30 cm); **S**: 8 in (45 cm)
❄❄❄ ◊ ◔ ☼ ☼

Sedum **(Herbstfreude Group) "Autumn Fire"**
This is one of the toughest and most reliable of perennials, looking its finest in the fall, when it produces its deep pink flowers, that turn gradually to a darker shade of red. Its succulent stems are attractive year-round.

H: 24 in (60 cm); **S**: 24 in (60 cm)
❄❄❄ ◊ ☼

Viburnum **x** *bodnantense* **"Dawn"**
Although this plant has good autumn leaf color, it is after leaf fall that it comes into its own. During the winter in some zones, it produces cluster after cluster of highly scented pink flowers. Enliven its summer clothing by growing a clematis in its branches.

H: 10 ft (3 m); **S**: 6 ft (2 m)
❄❄❄ ◊ ◔ ☼ ☼

Sturdy plants (Au–Gr)

Aucuba japonica "Crotonifolia"
This plant is one of the best for bringing a splash of color to the darkest of corners. Its leaves are spotted with pale markings which are brighter in better light, but still light up in the darker parts. Its evergreen leaves are tough and flexible.

H: 10 ft (3 m); **S**: 10 ft (3 m)
❄❄❄ ◊ ☀ ☀ ☀

Bergenia
Most perennials are of a delicate nature and won't take much abuse, but bergenia has big, leathery leaves that bounce back and clumps form a dense ground cover. Flowers are produced in spring and in winter the leaves turn shades of purple and red.

H: 6–24 in (15–60 cm); **S**: 8–24 in (20–60 cm) ❄❄❄ ◊ ☀ ☀

Brachyglottis "Sunshine Improved"
Its moundlike shape and yielding habit makes this a useful plant for growing at the edge of a border. It has soft gray leaves and produces small yellow flowers. Lightly cut it back every few years, in spring, to help it keep its shape.

H: 5 ft (1.5 m); **S**: 6 ft (2 m)
❄❄ ◊ ☀

Buxus sempervirens
Box is amenable to shaping and clipping into whatever form you wish. A small hedge of this separating lawn from border will deflect footballs and take most batterings without looking any the worse for it. Broken branches can be replaced with careful pruning.

H: 15 ft (5 m); **S**: 15 ft (5 m)
❄❄❄ ◊ ☀ ♈

Carex flagellifera
If there is any group of plants that can always be relied upon to spring back into shape after a trampling, it is grasses and sedges. Carex flagellifera has bronze foliage which, in mild climates, is held on the plant all year round, so it always looks good.

H: 3½ ft (1.1 m); **S**: 36 in (90 cm)
❄❄❄ ◊ ◊ ☀

Choisya ternata Sundance
This mounded, evergreen shrub has pale yellow foliage that lights up the garden. It has citrus-scented flowers in early summer (hence its common name Mexican orange blossom). The leaves have an attractive shiny surface and are spicily scented when crushed.

H: 8 ft (2.5 m); **S**: 8 ft (2.5 m)
❄❄❄ ◊ ◊ ☀ ♈

Cordyline australis
Cordylines quickly grow into impressive palmlike specimens. They can put on 6 ft (2 m) of growth in six years and have sturdy stems that occasionally branch. The straplike leaves look spiky, but are actually soft to the touch.

H: 10–30 ft (3–10 m); **S**: 3–12 ft (1–4 m) ❄❄ ◊ ☼ ☼ ♈

Cotoneaster horizontalis
This is a common plant that is easily overlooked, but it is tough and attractive, spreading its herringbone network of stems over walls or the ground. A profusion of berries in late summer is followed by excellent fall color. Good for wildlife.

H: 3 ft (1 m); **S**: 5 ft (1.5 m) ❄❄❄ ◊ ☼ ♈

Elaeagnus x ebbingei "Limelight"
This evergreen shrub has attractively yellow- and silver-variegated waxy leaves. It would form a good informal hedge or be useful in the back of a border. Scented flowers are produced in winter. Remove any all-green stems that appear once they have matured.

H: 12 ft (4 m); **S**: 12 ft (4 m) ❄❄❄ ◊ ☼ ☼

Erigeron karvinskianus
This pretty little plant is surprisingly tough, living happily in the cracks in pavement and walls, even where parts of it are regularly trampled and brushed against. It is a particularly useful plant for seeding into ugly cracks to give pavement a makeover.

H: 6–12 in (15–30 cm); **S**: 3 ft (1 m) ❄❄❄ ◊ ☼ ♈

Geranium "Johnson's Blue"
This is a large, sprawling hardy geranium smothered in beautiful purple-blue flowers all summer and well into the fall. At the edge of a border it will soften edges and keep down weeds. Cut it back hard after the first flush of flowers.

H: 12–18 in (30–45 cm); **S**: 24–30 in (60–75 cm) ❄❄❄ ◊ ◊ ♦ ☼ ☼ ☼ ♈

Griselinia littoralis "Variegata"
This plant has a soft mounded shape and thick, rounded, leathery leaves with cream markings. It is a great plant for using near the sea and in windy spots, and its pliable nature also makes it useful in places where it may sustain accidental damage.

H: 10 ft (3 m); **S**: 6 ft (2 m) ❄❄❄ ◊ ☼ ♈

Sturdy plants (Ha–Vi)

Hakonechloa macra "Aureola"
This grass has vivid yellow and pale green variegated leaves and an arching shape that will not be ruined by a few broken stems. It is one of the most compact of the ornamental grasses. It looks good in a container, but is equally happy in the ground.

H: 14 in (35 cm); **S**: 6 in (40 cm)
❄❄❄ ◊ ◔ ☼ ◐ ♈

Hebe "Red Edge"
This small hebe forms a low mound and makes an unusual edging plant, although it is better planted informally at the border edge, rather than as a hedge. Its succulent leaves have a red outline and the shoot tip takes on a pink tone in winter.

H: 18 in (45 cm); **S**: 24 in (60 cm)
❄❄ ◊ ◔ ☼ ◐ ♈

Lavandula angustifolia "Hidcote"
This is one of the more compact lavenders and is the best for use as an edging plant. It has vibrant, beautifully scented flowers. To maintain its shape, cut off the flowers as soon as they have faded and lightly trim the whole plant in spring.

H: 24 in (60 cm); **S**: 30 in (75 cm)
❄❄❄ ◊ ☼ ♈

Liriope muscari
This plant, commonly known as lilyturf, is one of the few bulbs tough enough to be used for edging. It is quick to colonize, making a very effective ground cover. It has a neat habit and arching green leaves, and in spring produces purple flowers.

H: 12 in (30 cm); **S**: 18 in (45 cm)
❄❄❄ ◊ ◔ ☼ ◐ ♈

Nepeta "Six Hills Giant"
This aromatic Mediterranean shrub makes a loose informal edging plant. Its foliage is strongly scented when crushed, so it is good to place it near a well-used path. Flowers attractive to insects cover the plant throughout summer and early fall.

H: 36 in (90 cm); **S**: 24 in (60 cm)
❄❄❄ ◊ ☼ ◐

Olearia macrodonta
This windbreak plant is often grown near the sea because of its tolerance to salt spray and its flexible stems. Those stems also come in handy where plants may suffer accidental damage. It is an elegant evergreen shrub with gray-green leaves.

H: 20 ft (6 m); **S**: 15 ft (5 m)
❄❄❄ ◊ ☼ ♈

Phormium tenax

New Zealand flax is one of the toughest of all plants and provides a bold outline all year round, with its arching, sword-shaped leaves. As well as the impressive specimens for the back of the border, there are several more compact cultivars.

H: 12 ft (4 m); **S**: 6 ft (2 m)
❀❀ ◊ ◑ ☼

Phyllostachys nigra **f.** henonis

All bamboos are sturdy, but the culms of this one are particularly tough and pliable, allowing them to bend in strong winds. It differs from *P. nigra* in having green culms that never turn black. They are also thicker and grow taller.

H: 10–15 ft (3–5 m); **S**: 6–10 ft (2–3 m) ❀❀❀ ◊ ◑ ☼ ◑ ♀

Santolina chamaecyparissus

This plant, commonly known as cotton lavender, forms a small, neat mound of grey feathery foliage and is good for edges. It grows well in coastal conditions, and the foliage is aromatic. In summer, small button-like yellow flowers cover the plant.

H: 20 in (50 cm); **S**: 3 ft (1 m)
❀❀ ◊ ☼ ♀

Sarcococca confusa

This robust, slow-growing evergreen is nothing to get excited about in summer, although the leaves are an attractive glossy deep green. It is in winter that it shines as it produces myriad tiny honey-scented flowers that can fill a garden with fragrance.

H: 6 ft (2 m); **S**: 3 ft (1 m)
❀❀❀ ◊ ◑ ☼ ◑ ♀

Stipa tenuissima

Once *Stipa tenuissima* makes itself at home it will reseed endlessly, cropping up all over the garden. Its presence is so light and airy that it never makes a pest of itself and, even better, it will not be damaged by being regularly brushed against.

H: 24 in (60 cm); **S**: 12 in (30 cm)
❀❀❀ ◊ ☼

Vinca major "Variegata"

This is a great plant for brightening up dull corners as it has cream and green foliage, purple star-shaped flowers, and will put up with even the deepest shade. It is a good ground cover plant, being particularly useful for binding soil on sloping sites.

H: 18 in (45 cm); **S**: indefinite
❀❀❀ ◊ ☼ ◑ ● ♀

Easy quick-flowering annuals

Amaranthus caudatus
Love-lies-bleeding is a fantastically exotic looking plant, yet flowers from seed in one season. The cascading ropes of flowers make it a fascinating plant for children to grow. Sow seed indoors in early spring or outdoors once all danger of frost has passed.

H: 3–5 ft (1–1.5 m); **S**: 18–30 in (45–75 cm) ❄❄ ◊ ☼

Centaurea cyanus
Cornflower has vibrant blue flowers borne on wiry stems. This is a hardy annual, and so can be sown direct into the soil. Sowing in the fall can produce larger plants and more flowers the following year. Deadhead regularly to prolong the display.

H: 8–32 in (20–80 cm); **S**: 6 in (15 cm) ❄❄❄ ◊ ◊ ☼ ☼

Cosmos bipinnatus "Sonata Pink"
The plant's large pink flowers float on delicate stems above ferny foliage. Annual cosmos makes a great filler for borders lacking in flower and its height makes it a good cut flower. Sow indoors in spring or outdoors when all danger of frost has passed.

H: 5 ft (1.5 m); **S**: 18 in (45 cm) ❄◊ ◊ ☼

Eschscholzia californica
This hardy annual is one of the best self-seeders: once it has grown in your garden one year, it will pop up thereafter with no intervention. Slender, graceful stems hold vivid orange flowers, which are a magnet for insects. Sow *in situ* in spring.

H: 12 in (30 cm); **S**: 6 in (15 cm) ❄❄❄ ◊ ☼ ♈

Helianthus
Few plants are more impressive to a child's eye than the sunflower. Held on tall stems, the huge flowers and bright colors appeal equally to many adults. They need a little cosseting to do their best. Sow in spring indoors, and transplant regularly.

H: 15 ft (5 m); **S**: 24 in (6 cm) ❄❄❄ ◊ ◊ ☼

Ipomoea purpurea
Stems romp up supports in one season and produce purple trumpet-shaped flowers. These are tender annuals, so need to be sown indoors, in a warm place and seedlings planted out once all chance of frost has passed.

H: 6–10 ft (2–3 m) ❄◊ ☼

Lathyrus odoratus
Sweet peas are good for adding height to borders, clothing a trellis or bamboo wigwam in one season. Those with larger flowers (such as the "Spencer" series) are often not the best scented so grow with simpler scented forms such as "Cupani."

H: 6 ft (2 m)
❄❄❄ ◊ ☼

Moluccella laevis
This is one of the more impressive plants that you can grow as an annual, forming 2 ft (60 cm)-high spikes of bell-shaped "flowers" (the true flowers are in the center). It makes a good cut flower and dries beautifully. Sow *in situ*, in spring.

H: 24–36 in (60–90 cm);
S: 9 in (23 cm) ❄◊ ◊ ☼

Salvia viridis
It is the colorful bracts that make this annual stand out, rather than its insignificant flowers. They are colored shades of purple and pink, and last very well when cut. Very easy and quick to grow from seed, which should be sown in spring.

H: 18–20 in (45–50 cm);
S: 9 in (23 cm) ❄❄❄ ◊ ☼

Tagetes
The brightly colored French marigold forms a cushion of foliage. Their strongly scented foliage makes them among the best plants for growing near vegetables as companion plants to deter pests. Sow direct in spring and deadhead often.

H: 8–10 in (20–30 cm);
S: 12 in (30 cm) ❄◊ ☼

Tropaeolum majus **Alaska Series**
Nasturtiums must be one of the easiest annuals, simply needing popping into the ground in spring and watering occasionally. The Alaska Series rewards this little effort with mounds of circular leaves and orange, red, yellow and cream flowers.

H: 3–10 ft (1–3 m); **S**: 5–15 ft
(1.5–5 m) ❄◊ ◊ ☼ ♔

Zinnia
Zinnias are excellent annuals with which to extend flowering into fall. They are often brightly colored and useful as cut flowers, and look somewhat dahlialike. Sow indoors in early spring or *in situ* from late spring.

H: 8–16 in (20–40 cm); **S**: 12 in
(30 cm) ❄◊ ☼

Easy edibles

Fava beans
Fava beans are simple to sow: just push the huge seeds into the ground and they will grow, you don't even need to cultivate the soil to a fine tilth. They germinate, grow, and crop quickly. Sow in fall and pinch out the tips in spring to prevent blackfly.

H: 36 in (90 cm); **S**: 10 in (25 cm)
❄❄❄ ◊ ◐ ☼

Calabrese
Calabrese is the quickest of the brassicas, ready to eat just a few months after sowing. It is also compact, so useful for smaller plots. Sow seeds in modules in early spring, planting them out when weather improves, or sow direct in late spring.

H: 36 in (90 cm); **S**: 20 in (50 cm)
❄ ◊ ◐ ☼

Carrots
Carrots can be eaten at any stage of their lives, but children particularly love them when they are tiny and sweet. Sow either little and often to get a constant supply of baby carrots, or sow a row and eat the thinnings, leaving the remainder to mature.

H: 6 in (15 cm); **S**: 6 in (15 cm)
❄❄❄ ◊ ☼

Zucchini
Zucchini make the ideal beginner's plant as they produce huge crops with little effort. They are tender, so sow seeds indoors in early spring and plant once all danger of frost has passed. Alternatively, buy plants from the nursery in early summer.

H: 3 ft (1 m); **S**: 3 ft (1 m)
❄ ◊ ◐ ☼

Lettuce
The speed at which lettuces grow is always impressive. Most tempting of all are baby leaves, for which you should sow over a wide drill. Cut the small plants with scissors, but leaving an inch of growth so that they can grow back.

H: 8–10 in (20–25 cm); **S**: 10–14 in (25–36 cm) ❄❄❄ ◊ ◐ ☼

New potatoes
Digging up potatoes, finding hidden treasure under that mound of foliage, will always be a magical experience. New potatoes are the tastiest—and quickest—of the lot. Allow seed potatoes to sprout (chit) in light, cool conditions and plant in early spring.

H: 3 ft (1 m); **S**: 3 ft (1 m)
❄❄❄ ◊ ◐ ☼

Peas

Peas are lovely fresh from the pod, but they are big plants and prey to many pests. Snow peas are much easier, and they have a sweetness and crunch that is appealing to children. Sow a small amount every few weeks from spring to midsummer.

H: 6 ft (1.8 m)
❄❄❄ ◊ ◑ ☼

Pumpkins

Pumpkins can be carved at halloween and you can spark a child's competitive instinct by trying to grow a giant to show off at the county fair. Plants are tender so sow seeds indoors in spring and plant out once danger of frost has passed.

H: 3 ft (1 m); **S**: 10 ft (3 m)
❄ ◊ ◑ ☼

Spring onions

Spring onions are the quickest of the onions, and are also relatively mild and palatable to children. They take up little space in the vegetable garden. Sow directly where they are to grow in spring, thinning out after seeds have germinated.

H: 8 in (20 cm); **S**: 1 in (2.5 cm)
❄❄❄ ◊ ◑ ☼

Strawberries

Make sure that strawberries are planted in your sunniest spot and try to prevent eager hands from picking them to soon. The rule is: when you think they are ready, leave them for one more day. Protect the plants well from slugs and other pests.

H: 6 in (15 cm); **S**: 12 in (30 cm)
❄❄❄ ◊ ☼

Sweetcorn

Sweetcorn is a favorite vegetable of many children, who love the novelty of eating them off the cob. Sweetcorn needs sowing indoors in spring and planting out once all danger of frost has passed. Plant in a block, as flowers are wind-pollinated.

H: 6 ft (1.8 m); **S**: 12 in (30 cm)
❄ ◊ ☼

Tomatoes

There is a huge variety of tomatoes available, and the bite-sized cherry tomatoes are especially popular. These also have the benefit of maturing early and can miss the worst of blight. Look out for stripy-skinned heirloom cultivars.

H: 6 ft (1.8 m); **S**: 24 in (60 cm)
❄ ◊ ◑ ☼

Scented plants

Chamaemelum nobile "Treneague"
The delicious scent of chamomile is particularly strong when the leaves are touched or crushed underfoot. Because this is a low-growing plant, it is possible to make a chamomile lawn using the non-flowering "Treneague." Clip occasionally to keep neat.

H: 4 in (10 cm); **S**: 18 in (45 cm)
❊❊❊ ◊ ☼ ♛

Cosmos atrosanguineus
The chocolate plant got its name as the late summer flowers are chocolate scented, making them a hit with children in particular. Give the roots of this perennial a protective mulch over winter or lift and store in a frost-free place.

H: 30 in (75 cm); **S**: 18 in (45 cm)
❊❊ ◊ ◗ ☼ ♛

Lavandula stoechas
The lovely scent of lavender is created by oils in the foliage, released when the weather is warm or by crushing the leaves. French lavender has extra interest because of the pretty "bunny ears" petals on the tops of the flowers. Clip lightly after flowering.

H: 24 in (60 cm); **S**: 24 in (60 cm)
❊❊❊ ◊ ☼ ♛

Lonicera periclymenum "Serotina"
The late Dutch honeysuckle is a vigorous climber, clamboring up any support it is given, from where it will fill the mid- to late summer evenings with scent. The outsides of the flowers are red, which shows off the pale inner parts well.

H: 22 ft (7 m)
❊❊❊ ◊ ☼ ◗ ♛

Matthiola incana Brompton Series
Brompton stocks are among the most highly scented of all plants, and they produce attractive flowers in a good range of colors. Grow as annuals from an early spring sowing or, for more success, sow in midsummer for flowers the following year.

H: 32 in (80 cm); **S**: 16 in (40 cm)
❊❊❊ ◊ ◗ ☼ ♛

Melissa officinalis
The fresh young foliage of lemon balm is not only deliciously lemon scented, but it also tastes good and is useful in teas and desserts. As the plant starts to flower, the taste is less good, but it then becomes a magnet for bees and other insects.

H: 2–4 ft (60–120 cm); **S**: 12–18 in (30–45 cm) ❊❊❊ ◊ ☼ ♛

Mentha suaveolens **"Variegata"**
Like all mints, this cultivar has a strong scent. Its predominant fragrance, when lightly brushed, is of pineapple, hence its common name —pineapple mint. It is not as vigorous as other mints, but still grow it in a container and not the open ground.

H: 3 ft (1 m); **S**: indefinite
❄❄❄ ◐ ☼ ♈

Pelargonium crispum **"Variegatum"**
Scented-leaved pelargoniums have many different scents, from cinnamon to mint. This one has a lemon scent when crushed. Pelargoniums are not hardy and, in cold zones, need to be overwintered in a cool, bright place, such as a porch or greenhouse.

H: 14–18 in (35–45 cm); **S**: 5–6 in (12–15 cm) ❄◊ ☼ ♈

Philadelphus **"Manteau d'Hermine"**
Philadelphus is a deciduous shrub that produces deliciously orange-scented flowers in midsummer. "Manteau d'Hermine" is a compact cultivar, making it perfect for smaller gardens and yards. Prune after flowering, removing the oldest stems.

H: 30 in (75 cm); **S**: 5 ft (1.5 m)
❄❄❄ ◊ ☼ ◐ ♈

Rosa **"Zéphirine Drouhin"**
This famous old rose has vibrant pink flowers with a strong scent. It can be grown as a climber or shrub, and it has thornless stems, making pruning easy. However, it can be prone to disease, so you might consider *R.* "Gertrude Jekyll" in its place.

H: 10 ft (3 m); **S**: 6 ft (2 m)
❄❄❄ ◊ ◐ ☼ ♈

Thymus citriodorus
Lemon-scented thyme has tiny, dark green, strongly scented leaves and pink flowers that are borne in summer. Growth stays low and it slowly spreads. It makes an excellent culinary herb and should be regularly pinched out for bushy growth.

H: 12 in (30 cm); **S**: 10 in (25 cm)
❄❄❄ ◊ ☼ ♈

Trachelospermum jasminoides
This elegant climber twines around fences and trellises, clothing them in dark, glossy leaves year round. In summer, small, white, star-shaped flowers are produced, which fill the evening air with a jasmine scent. It does best in a sunny, sheltered corner.

H: 28 ft (9 m)
❄❄ ◊ ☼ ◐ ♈

Noisy plants

Betula pendula
The stems of the weeping birch knock and brush against each other in the wind, making this a good plant to help distract from traffic noise. Plant birch trees in fall or winter and stake for up to three years while the roots get established.

H: 80 ft (25 m); **S**: 30 ft (10 m)
❄❄❄ ◊ ◖ ☼ ☀ ☀ ♛

Briza maxima
The quaking grass has small heads of flowers that nod gracefully on the tops of slender stems. As the seeds inside mature, the seed heads turn papery and rustle in the slightest breeze. This is an annual that should be sown each year in spring.

H: 18–24 in (45–60 cm); **S**: 10 in (25 cm) ❄❄❄ ◊ ☼

Lunaria annua "Variegata"
Honesty has purple, fragrant flowers in spring, which are a boon for wildlife, being nectar rich. Once the flowers have faded, unusual round and flat seedheads form. They are green at first, but turn translucent and papery, rustling to the touch.

H: 36 in (90 cm); **S**: 12 in (30 cm)
❄❄❄ ◊ ◖ ☼ ☀

Milium effusum "Aureum"
This golden grass has soft, pliable leaves that make a subtle whisper in a breeze. It is a wonderful plant for lighting up dark corners, as it keeps its color in shade, only turning pale green as the plant matures. Divide in spring every few years.

H: 24 in (60 cm); **S**: 12 in (30 cm)
❄❄❄ ◊ ◖ ☀ ♛

Miscanthus sinensis
Miscanthus is a tall grass with narrow, arching leaves and feathery flower plumes that brush together in the wind. The flower plumes are produced in late summer and if left on the plant all winter, they provide good seasonal interest.

H: 12 ft (4 m); **S**: 4 ft (1.2 m)
❄❄❄ ◊ ◖ ☼

Nandina domestica
Run your hand through heavenly bamboo's leaves (despite its name it isn't related to bamboo) to hear a satisfying dry rustling sound. The evergreen leaves emerge coppery pink in spring, turn green, and then red and purple in cold weather.

H: 6 ft (2 m); **S**: 5 ft (1.5 m)
❄❄ ◊ ◖ ☀ ♛

Nigella damascena

Love-in-a-mist is one of the easiest annuals to grow and, once established, re-seeds itself year after year. Once the blue flowers go over, fat, round seedheads are formed and the seeds rattle inside these pods once they are mature.

H: 20 in (50 cm); **S**: 9 in (23 cm)
❄❄❄ ◊ ☼

Papaver somniferum

Opium poppy produces tall stems topped by impressive large, silky flowers. It re-seeds itself easily every year once established. After flowering, seedheads are formed and the seeds rattle inside. The seed is that used on bread and rolls.

H: 4 ft (1.2 m); **S**: 12 in (30 cm)
❄❄❄ ◊ ☼

Pennisetum alopecuroides

Wind whispers through the soft flower plumes of fountain grass, which produces its soft, translucent bristles of flowers in late summer. They will stand over winter, for seasonal interest. Cut the remaining stems down to the ground in spring.

H: 2–5 ft (0.6–1.5 m); **S**: 2–4 ft (0.6–1.2 m) ❄❄ ◊ ☼

Phyllostachys nigra

Black bamboo is particularly distinctive, with its jet-black stems showing off mid-green leaves. Like all bamboos, it makes a magical sound in the yard, the leaves swishing in the breeze and the stems making a hollow noise as they knock together.

H: 10–15 ft (3–5 m); **S**: 6–10 ft (2–3 m) ❄❄❄ ◊ ◑ ☼ ◐ ☗

Physalis alkekengi "Chinese Lantern"

Physalis produces tiny white flowers in summer, but it is the fall seedheads that the plant is grown for. They form large, bright orange, balloonlike lanterns and turn papery and rustly. They gradually fade and leave an intricate skeleton.

H: 24–30 in (60–75 cm); **S**: 36 in (90 cm) ❄❄❄ ◊ ☼ ◐ ☗

Platycodon grandiflorus

Platycodon is known as the balloon flower. The flowerbuds are large and swollen, like a balloon, but they also make a popping sound when squeezed. This is a low growing herbaceous perennial or alpine plant that gives good late summer color.

H: 24 in (60 cm); **S**: 12 in (30 cm)
❄❄❄ ◊ ◑ ☼ ◐ ☗

Tactile plants

Alchemilla mollis
Ladies mantle has soft, felty leaves. They emerge fresh and new in spring, and are followed by a froth of yellow flowers in summer. Alchemilla often self-seeds into the tiniest of patches of soil, and can be a lovely plant for softening patios.

H: 24 in (60 cm); **S**: 30 in (75 cm)
❋❋❋ ◊ ☼ ◑ ☀ ♀

Antirrhinum
Snapdragons are magical plants for children. Plucked off a stem, a flower opens and closes its mouth with a soft pinch to either side of it. They are also colorful bedding plants, sown in spring under cover and planted out or direct where they are to grow.

H: 6 in–4 ft (15 cm–1.2 m);
S: 6–24 in (15–60 cm) ❋❋❋ ◊ ☼

Arbutus unedo
This evergreen small tree or large shrub bears small white fall flowers and strawberry-shaped fruit. The textural interest is in the bark, which is cinammon colored when the plant is young, and reddish, craggy and shredding when older.

H: 25 ft (8 m); **S**: 25 ft (8 m)
❋❋❋ ◊ ☼ ♀

Artemesia "Powis Castle"
Artemesia has feathery silver foliage that is soft to the touch and aromatic. It does flower, but they are tiny and insignificant and don't distract from the foliage. Use as a background to strongly colored or pastel plants. Provide the best possible drainage.

H: 24 in (60 cm); **S**: 36 in (90 cm)
❋❋ ◊ ☼ ♀

Corylus avellana "Contorta"
The impossible twists and turns of the corkscrew hazel invite exploring hands. The spiraling growth makes this a slow-growing shrub, easily containable. The stems are at their best in early spring when the show of dead straight catkins appears.

H: 15 ft (5 m); **S**: 15 ft (5 m)
❋❋❋ ◊ ☼ ◑

Foeniculum vulgare
Fennel foliage is soft and feathery and has a strong aniseed flavor that some—but by no means all—children love. It is a perennial herb that will die down in winter and reappear in spring. Both foliage and seeds can be used in cooking.

H: 6 ft (1.8 m); **S**: 18 in (45 cm)
❋❋❋ ◊ ◑ ☼

Phlomis fruticosa
The Jerusalem sage has gray-green leaves that are aromatic when rubbed. It bears whorls of bright yellow flowers in summer and the seedheads look good in fall. Cut out frost damage in spring, and lightly trim back the plant all over.

H: 3 ft (1 m); **S**: 5 ft (1.5 m)
❄❄❄ ◊ ☼ ♈

Prunus serrula
This lovely small tree has peeling, copper-colored bark punctuated by narrow rough stripes. When in close proximity it is hard to resist a stroke. The bark is particularly prominent in winter. In spring, the tree has fairly insignificant white blossoms.

H: 30 ft (10 m); **S**: 30 ft (10 m)
❄❄❄ ◊ ◐ ☼ ♈

Salvia argentea
This sage relative is grown for its huge, soft, felty leaves. They are wonderfully soft to the touch, silvery-gray and glistening. Remove the pinkish-white flowers when they first appear or they will cause the quality of the foliage to deteriorate.

H: 36 in (90 cm); **S**: 24 in (60 cm)
❄❄❄ ◊ ◐ ☼ ◐ ☼ ♈

Senecio cineraria
This plant is grown for its silvery leaves, which are covered in hundreds of tiny white hairs, making the plant soft to the touch. It is most often grown as an annual and is an excellent foil for brightly colored annual flowers.

H: 24 in (60 cm); **S**: 24 in (60 cm)
❄❄ ◊ ☼

Stachys byzantina "Lamb's Ear"
This plant is a wonderful border edging plant, producing huge, felty, silver-gray leaves that lap over paths. It does flower, but the felty, purple flowers are fairly small. This cultivar has larger but less silvery leaves than the species.

H: 18 in (45 cm); **S**: 24 in (60 cm)
❄❄❄ ◊ ☼

Stipa gigantea
The flower plumes and later seedheads produce a golden haze, hence its common name—golden oat grass. It is a good plant for adding height to a border. Leave growth on the plant over winter, where it will catch low winter light.

H: 8 ft (2.5 m); **S**: 4 ft (1.2 m)
❄❄❄ ◊ ☼ ♈

Bold and colorful plants

Agapanthus "Blue Giant"
These herbaceous perennials are as happy in a pot as in a border; in fact, they may even flower better when their roots are restricted. They produce impressive blue, purple, or white heads of flowers. Hardy types include "Castle of Mey" or "Lilliput."

H: 4 ft (1.2 m); **S**: 24 in (60 cm)
❄❄❄ ◐ ◑ ☼

Allium giganteum
Big, beautiful pompoms of purple flowers are borne at the tops of tall stems in early summer. They seem to float above the border, and perfectly complement herbaceous plants and roses. Clumps will gradually grow and occasionally need splitting.

H: 5–6 ft (1.5–2 m); **S**: 6 in (15 cm)
❄❄❄ ◐ ☼ ♔

Beta vulgaris subsp. cicla "Bright Lights"
The rainbow stems of this chard make a wonderfully ornamental feature in a vegetable garden. They are edible, but the stems come in a range of colors, including reds, yellows, and oranges. Sow seed direct, in spring.

H: 9 in (23 cm); **S**: 18 in (45 cm)
❄❄❄ ◐ ☼ ☀ ♔

Calendula officinalis "Art Shades"
Marigold "Art Shades" has double flowers in shades of apricot, pale yellow, and cream, as well as the usual bright orange. For large plants and lots of flowers, sow seed direct in mid- to late summer for a show the following year.

H: 12–28 in (30–70 cm); **S**: 12–18 in (30–45 cm) ❄❄❄ ◐ ☼ ☀

Callistemon citrinus "Splendens"
Bottle brush, as this Australian plant is commonly known, is aptly named. The red flowers are wrapped around the stems and have long, protruding, yellow-tipped stamens. The lemon-scented leaves grow along the stem as if the flowers never happened.

H: 6–25 ft (2–8 m); **S**: 5–20 ft (1.5–6 m) ❄◐ ◑ ☼ ♔

Canna "Richard Wallace"
None of the cannas are subtle plants, but "Richard Wallace" is particularly eye-catching. Its large, bright green bananalike leaves are the perfect foil for the flamboyant flowers. Cannas need winter protection, so in fall, mulch or dig up and move indoors.

H: 5 ft (1.5 m); **S**: 20 in (50 cm)
❄◐ ☼

Crocosmia "Lucifer"

The flowers of *Crocosmia* "Lucifer" are a hot orange-red and are borne through mid- and late summer. This is a very tough plant, hardy in cold conditions and tolerant of winds and salt-spray. As a result, it can be a bit thuggish in less stressful conditions.

H: 3–4 ft (1–1.2 m); **S**: 3 in (8 cm)
❄❄❄ ◊ ◊ ☼ ☼ ♈

Hedychium coccineum

With its straplike evergreen leaves and whorls of exotic scented orange flowers at the top of tall stems, the ginger lily brings a truly subtropical look to temperate gardens. Plants are root hardy once established, so mulch thickly in winter.

H: 10 ft (3 m); **S**: 3 ft (1 m)
❄◊ ◊ ☼ ☼ ♈

Impatiens niamniamensis

This quirky little plant has brightly bi-colored flowers that hang beneath the foliage like clusters of little parrots. It can be grown outside in summer, but is completely tender and will need bringing indoors before the first frosts.

H: 36 in (90 cm); **S**: 14 in (35 cm)
❄◊ ◊ ☼

Kniphofia uvaria "Nobilis"

This is a tall, striking perennial with spires of brightly colored, tubelike flowers. "Nobilis" is a particularly tall-growing cultivar, and has huge, fat flowerheads. It flowers in late summer and looks particularly good among tall-growing grasses.

H: 4 ft (1.2 m); **S**: 24 in (60 cm)
❄❄❄ ◊ ◊ ☼ ☼ ♈

Osteospermum

The daisylike flowers of osteospermum are produced all summer and in many colors. These half-hardy perennials make fantastic bedding plants for containers. Keep plants well watered to prevent them from going into dormancy.

H: 4–24 in (10–60 cm); **S**: 18–36 in (45–90 cm) ❄❄ ◊ ☼ ♈

Solenostemon scutellarioides

The leaves of coleus are splashed with bold shades of red, yellow, brown, pink, and purple. There is barely a drop of green on some of them. Grow as annuals or over winter indoors, keeping almost dry in cool, bright, frost-free conditions.

H: 24–30 in (60–75 cm); **S**: 24–30 in (60–75 cm) ❄◊ ◊ ☼ ☼

Plants to attract wildlife

Buddleja davidii "Fascinating"

Buddlejas are so popular with butterflies they have gained the common name of butterfly bush. The flowers contain a large amount of nectar, and with their large flowerheads are easy for butterflies to land on and feed from.

H: 10 ft (3 m); **S**: 15 ft (5 m)
❄❄❄ ◊ ☼

Crataegus monogyna

Hawthorn makes a fine hedge or small tree and it is one of the best plants for wildlife. The nectar-rich flowers signify summer has truly arrived. The hips are eaten by birds and small mammals and its branches are sought after as nesting sites.

H: 30 ft (10 m); **S**: 25 ft (8 m)
❄❄❄ ◊ ◑ ☼ ◐

Echinops ritro

Bees, moths, and butterflies all flock to these blue, round, thistlelike flowers, and the seeds are eaten by seed-eating birds such as finches. The plant strikes an architectural pose in a border, and the attractive seedheads persist over winter.

H: 24 in (60 cm); **S**: 18 in (45 cm)
❄❄❄ ◊ ☼

Hedera helix

The common ivy is one of the best plants for wildlife, providing shelter and nest sites for birds, and important winter pollen and berries. It will only flower and fruit once growth switches from juvenile climbing phase to the mature phase.

H: 30 ft (10 m)
❄❄❄ ◊ ◑ ☼ ◐

Leucanthemum vulgare

The oxeye daisy is a simple flower with lovely clear white petals with yellow centers borne on tall stems. It is as attractive to insects as it is to gardeners. It is particularly at home in meadow-style plantings. It flowers from early summer into fall.

H: 12–36 in (30–90 cm); **S**: 24 in (60 cm) ❄❄ ◊ ☼

Limnanthes douglasii

This is one of the best plants for companion planting, as it is extremely attractive to hoverflies (the larvae of which eat aphids) and bees (fantastic pollinators). It has low, sprawling growth and large "poached egg" flowers. Grow from seed each year.

H: 6 in (15 cm); **S**: 6 in (15 cm)
❄❄❄ ◊ ◑ ☼ ◐ ♈

Primula vulgaris

The simple flowers of primulas provide nectar early in the year, when there are few other flowers around (avoid growing double forms, as these make nectar less available). The leaves form small rosettes from which are borne the delicate yellow flowers.

H: 8 in (20 cm); **S**: 14 in (35 cm)
❄❄❄ ◊ ☀ ⚇ ♛

Pyracantha "Mohave"

Insects visit the flowers of pyracantha, but it is for their fall and winter berries that they are most useful in the wildlife garden, as birds love them. These are tough and easy plants and totally unfussy about soil, providing wonderful winter interest.

H: 12 ft (4 m); **S**: 15 ft (5 m)
❄❄ ◊ ☀ ⚇

Rosa rugosa

This vigorous hedging rose bears bright pink flowers all summer long, which are attractive to insects. These are followed by large, orange-red hips, which are not a favorite food for birds, but they make a good emergency standby.

H: 3–8 ft (1–2.5 m); **S**: 3–8 ft (1–2.5 m) ❄❄❄ ◊ ◊ ☀

Rosmarinus officinalis "Roseus"

Rosemary is a great favorite of bees, and a large plant will be humming with visitors on a warm day. It is a Mediterranean plant so needs excellent drainage and a sunny, sheltered site. It has fragrant stems and makes a robust herb for cooking.

H: 5 ft (1.5 m); **S**: 5 ft (1.5 m)
❄❄ ◊ ☀

Sedum spectabile "Brilliant"

The many tiny flowers that cover a flowerhead of "Brilliant" are rich in nectar and are attractive to ladybugs, lacewings, and hoverflies. They produce this nectar late in the season, so are particularly useful for helping insects prepare themselves for winter.

H: 18 in (45 cm); **S**: 18 in (45 cm)
❄❄❄ ◊ ☀ ♛

Sorbus aucuparia

The rowan tree, or mountain ash, is a particularly tough tree, able to withstand high winds and exposed locations. It bears panicles of small flowers in spring and large, orange-red berries in fall loved by blackbirds and grosbeaks.

H: 50 ft (15 m); **S**: 22 ft (7 m)
❄❄❄ ◊ ☀ ⚇

Oversized plants

Cardiocrinum giganteum
This giant lily is a breathtaking sight, especially when flowers are planted *en masse*. The flowers have a familiar lilylike appearance, but the stems can reach up to 12 ft (4 m). Plants are raised from seed, but need several years to build up to flowering size.

H: 5–12 ft (1.5–4 m); **S**: 18 in (45 cm)
❄❄❄ ◊ ◐ ☀

Catalpa bignonioides
This is too large a tree for smaller gardens if left to grow naturally, but it loves to be pollarded annually in spring, which will keep it in bounds. This is also the way to get the best foliage, as each year it is hard pruned the leaves get more impressive.

H: 50 ft (15 m); **S**: 50 ft (15 m)
❄❄❄ ◊ ◐ ☀ ♔

Chusquea culeou
Although this is a tall-growing bamboo, it is also what is known as a "clumper," which means that its rhizomes do not run all over the yard, taking it over. The leaves radiate around the stems, giving a distinctive "foxtail" appearance.

H: 20 ft (6 m); **S**: 8 ft (2.5 m)
❄❄❄ ◊ ◐ ☀ ☼ ♔

Cyathea australis
This plant is known as the rough tree fern because of the texture of its stem. It can tolerate a slightly more exposed position than the more well-known *Dicksonia antarctica*. It needs plenty of moisture and winter protection to the crown.

H: 3–10 ft (1–3 m); **S**: 10–15 ft (3–5 m) ❄◊ ◐ ☼ ☀

Cynara cardunculus
Cardoon has a striking presence. It is tall and thistlelike, with beautiful, deeply-cut silver foliage. Buds and flowers are similar to those of artichokes and make a great winter feature if left on the plant. Clear away the old growth in early spring.

H: 5 ft (1.5 m); **S**: 4 ft (1.2 m)
❄❄❄ ◊ ☀ ♔

Dicksonia antarctica
Tree ferns create a magical, rain forestlike atmosphere in a shady spot. They grow extremely slowly, but you can buy large specimens for an instant jungle. It needs shelter, shadem and moisture; protect the crown in winter by stuffing it with straw.

H: 12 ft (4 m); **S**: 9 ft (2.7 m)
❄❄ ◊ ☀ ♔

x *Fatshedera lizei*

This inter-generic cross between an ivy and a fatsia has large, glossy, dark green palmate leaves somewhere between the size of its two parents. It has an ivy's climbing habit, but not its clinging power, so it doesn't damage walls but needs tying in to a support.

H: 4–6 ft (1.2–2 m); **S**: 10 ft (3 m)
❄❄ ◌ ◑ ☼ ☼ ⚘

Fatsia japonica

Fatsia is a wonderfully dramatic plant for your darkest and trickiest of spots. It has huge, glossy, dark green leaves that are at their best in a shady, sheltered situation. It may sometimes be hit hard by frost, the leaves going limp. They usually recover quickly.

H: 5–12 ft (1.5–4 m); **S**: 5–12 ft (1.5–4 m) ❄❄ ◌ ◑ ☼ ☼ ⚘

Gunnera manicata

The giant rhubarb is the ultimate oversized plant. The leaves on a mature clump can reach as much as 6 ft (2 m) across. The plant loves damp, and is best in a bog garden. Use the old leaves to protect the crown in winter.

H: 8 ft (2.5 m); **S**: 10–12 ft (3–4 m)
❄❄❄ ◑◑ ☼ ☼ ⚘

Musa basjoo

The Japanese banana quickly grows into a large clump topped with huge, paddlelike tropical leaves. Although it is root hardy (it will come back each spring), to get an impressive clump you need to protect the stems each winter, at least for the first few years.

H: 15 ft (5 m); **S**: 12 ft (4 m)
❄❄ ◌ ☼ ⚘

Rheum palmatum

This is a giant rhubarb that reaches nothing like the dimensions of *Gunnera manicata*, but it has big leaves nonetheless, and particularly attractive ones, green on top and purple underneath. It is best planted in a bog garden.

H: 8 ft (2.5 m); **S**: 6 ft (1.8 m)
❄❄❄ ◑ ☼ ☼

Trachycarpus fotunei

The Chusan palm grows slowly, but can reach an impressive height if planted in suitable conditions. This is the hardiest of the palms and one to plant for a large specimen. It prefers warmth and shelter, and can look tattered if planted in a windy spot.

H: 70 ft (20 m); **S**: 8 ft (2.5 m)
❄❄ ◌ ☼ ☼ ⚘

Plants for creating mini landscapes

Androsace carnea
This alpine plant has small, spreading shoots covered in tiny, spiky, gray-green leaves and has pink flowers in late spring. Place gravel around the stems of the plant and water from below to make sure that no water lies on the foliage.

H: 2 in (5 cm); **S**: 3–6 in (8–15 cm)
❋❋❋ ◊ ◑ ☼

Arenaria tetraquetra
This tiny alpine plant forms a ground hugging mat. From late spring it produces small, white, four-petaled flowers. It needs very sharp drainage, but should not be allowed to dry out. Place gravel around it to prevent the foliage from sitting in wet soil.

H: 1–2 in (2.5–5 cm); **S**: 6–8 in (15–20 cm) ❋❋❋ ◑ ☼

Asplenium ceterach
This lovely fern is tiny, and perfect for creating a miniature jungle effect. It naturally grows in and spreads along the cracks and fissures of walls in damp areas, but can be introduced. It has lobed foliage, which is a rusty orange on its back.

H: 6 in (15 cm); **S**: 8 in (20 cm)
❋❋❋ ◊ ◑ ☼

Campanula garganica
This is a low-growing creeping plant with trailing stems that are covered in star-shaped blue flowers throughout summer. Grow it at the edge of a trough and it will trail over and soften the planting. It needs sharp drainage and full sun to perform at its best.

H: 2 in (5 cm); **S**: 12 in (30 cm)
❋❋❋ ◊ ◑ ☼ ☼ ♈

Daphne petraea "Grandiflora"
This is an extremely slow growing dwarf shrub that gradually forms a low mound shape. Deep pink, strongly fragrant flowers smother the plant in spring, gradually fading to a pale pink. Grow in sharply drained soil and cover the surface in gravel.

H: 4 in (10 cm); **S**: 10 in (25 cm)
❋❋❋ ◊ ☼ ☼

Draba mollissima
This plant forms a little rounded hummock of rosettes of gray-green leaves. In late spring it is covered in small, bold yellow flowers. It enjoys alpine house conditions and shelter from excessive moisture during the winter. Do not wet the foliage.

H: 3 in (8 cm); **S**: 8 in (20 cm)
❋❋❋ ◊ ☼

Hebe ochracea "James Stirling"

This dwarf hebe would make a good foliage plant for a jungly miniature garden. It is an evergreen with golden-green coloring that is greener in summer and more bronze colored in winter, and so makes a good winter feature.

H: 18 in (45 cm); **S**: 24 in (60 cm)
❊❊❊ ◊ ◗ ☼ ◑ ♈

Raoulia hookeri

This alpine plant forms a dense mat of tiny, overlapping, silvery leaves. It has a wonderful texture, clinging close to the ground. Pale green flowers are produced in summer. Grow in sharply drained soil and protect from winter wet.

H: ½ in (1 cm); **S**: 8 in (20 cm)
❊❊ ◊ ◗ ☼ ◑

Salix apoda

This is a tiny shrub that will give an air of maturity and a little structure to a miniature garden or trough. It has a prostrate habit, and so looks good spilling over the edge of a container. Silver-gray catkins are its main attraction, borne in spring.

H: 8 in (20 cm); **S**: 24 in (60 cm)
❊❊❊ ◊ ◗ ☼

Saxifraga x irvingii

This plant forms a small, cushionlike mound of tiny rosettes of leaves. In early spring, flowers are produced, large in comparison with the plant. They are pale pink with darker insides. Likes well-drained soil, but should still be kept well watered.

H: 2 in (5 cm); **S**: 8 in (20 cm)
❊❊❊ ◊ ☼

Sedum acre

This is a tiny, mat-forming and sometimes trailing succulent plant. It grows naturally in crevices in walls and will be happy in a trough filled with well-drained soil. Throughout summer, it produces masses of star-shaped, yellow-green flowers.

H: 2 in (5 cm); **S**: 24 in (60 cm)
❊❊❊ ◊ ☼

Sempervivum tectorum

The clustering rosettes of the houseleek make this a very special plant for containers that need low growing plants as they form an intricately textured carpet of leaves. Reddish-purple flowers are produced in summer. Grow in well-drained soil.

H: 6 in (15 cm); **S**: 20 in (50 cm)
❊❊❊ ◊ ☼ ♈

Easy bulbs for planting

Camassia leichtlinii subsp. suksdorfii
This impressive spring bulb forms a spire of star-shaped white flowers. It grows well in clay soils, as it likes to be damp in spring and drier during its summer dormancy. Cut back after the leaves have started to turn yellow.

H: 24–54 in (60–130 cm); **S**: 4 in (10 cm) ❋❋ ◊ ◐ ☼ ☀

Convallaria majalis "Albostriata"
This is a variation on the classic lily-of-the-valley, with unusual crisp yellow lines along the foliage. It has the same strong, luxurious scent, but needs a little more sun to keep its variegation. The straight species will thrive in extremely low light.

H: 9 in (23 cm); **S**: 12 in (30 cm)
❋❋❋ ◊ ◐ ☼ ♛

Crocus "Gipsy Girl"
Crocus is one of the earliest bulbs of the year, and the bold coloring of "Gipsy Girl" will certainly liven up the early spring garden. The bright yellow flowers are striped in deep purple, and the insides are plain bright yellow. Grow in grass or borders.

H: 3 in (7 cm); **S**: 2 in (5 cm)
❋❋❋ ◊ ☼

Fritillaria meleagris
The nodding purple, bell-shaped flowers of snake's head fritillaries are covered in checkered patterning. They love to grow in rough grass in dappled shade, and clumps gradually increase. Plant in drifts and only cut grass once the foliage has died down.

H: 12 in (30 cm); **S**: 2–3 in (5–8 cm)
❋❋❋ ◊ ☼ ☀

Galtonia candicans
This beautiful summer bulb produces tall spires of gray-green leaves and hanging, waxy, white, bell-shaped flowers. It prefers sandy soils and may rot away where winters are damp. In ideal conditions it will seed itself around the garden.

H: 3–4 ft (1–1.2 m); **S**: 4 in (10 cm)
❋❋❋ ◊ ◐ ☼ ♛

Gladiolus communis subsp. byzantinus
This gladiolus is very different from the rigid, blowsy, florist types. It has delicate growth and searing magenta flowers and looks wonderful against silver or purple foliage. It spreads well, once established.

H: 3 ft (1 m); **S**: 3 in (8 cm)
❋❋❋ ◊ ☼ ♛

Hyacinthus orientalis

Hyacinths can produce flowers extremely early in the year and have a strong fragrance. Treated types can be forced for Christmas or early winter indoor displays and then planted out in the garden to bloom in future years.

H: 8–12 in (20–30 cm); **S**: 3 in (8 cm)
❄❄❄ ◊ ◖ ☼

Iris "Harmony"

This is a petite iris that produces its deep blue flowers with a dot of yellow on each petal in late winter. They thrust their arrow-straight green leaves up through bare soil and brighten up the garden when little else is flowering.

H: 4–6 in (10–15 cm)
❄❄❄ ◊ ☼ ◑

Lilium candidum

One of the few lilies that must be planted in fall, *Lilium candidum* produces a rosette of overwintering leaves. In summer, tall flower spikes are covered in up to 15 large, pure white, scented flowers, the scent particularly strong on warm evenings.

H: 3–6 ft (1–1.8 m)
❄❄❄ ◊ ☼ ♈

Narcissus "Tête-à-tête"

Daffodils are particularly easy bulbs. Dwarf forms such as "Tête-à-tête" are sturdy and bright. Their size makes them well suited to containers, but they can also be naturalized in rough grass. For the best show, plant daffodil bulbs in early fall.

H: 6 in (15 cm)
❄❄❄ ◊ ◖ ☼ ◑ ♈

Nectaroscordum siculum

Producing loose, hanging umbels of bell-shaped flowers, in antique shades of cream, dusky pink and soft green, this is an extremely refined plant. Plant bulbs in fall and they will self-seed. The dried seed pods are attractive in flower arrangements.

H: 4 ft (1.2 m); **S**: 4 in (10 cm)
❄❄❄ ◊ ☼ ◑

Tulipa "Spring Green"

The fresh, subtle coloring of this tulip allows it to be planted alongside many other tulips easily; it contrasts with dark colors or blends well with pastels. Plant in late fall as early planting can lead to premature growth during warm spells.

H: 16 in (40 cm)
❄❄❄ ◊ ☼ ♈

Plants for hayfever sufferers

Clematis "Nelly Moser"
Clematis are insect pollinated and so produce no irritating wind-blown pollen. "Nelly Moser" is one of the few suited to shade where its flowers' dark pink striping is at its strongest. The flowers are produced in early summer and often again in fall.

H: 6–10 ft (2–3 m); **S**: 3 ft (1 m)
❋❋❋ ◊ ☼ ◑ ☽ ♔

Cornus kousa var. chinensis
Wind-blown tree pollen is one of the most common causes of hayfever, but this dogwood is insect pollinated. It is a beautiful, large shrub or small tree for an acid soil. The "flowers" are actually large, showy bracts surrounding the tiny true flowers.

H: 22 ft (7 m); **S**: 15 ft (5 m)
❋❋❋ ◊ ☼ ◑ ♔

Cydonia oblonga
Any trees that produce blossom are insect pollinated and so no threat to hayfever sufferers, and the edible quince produces some of the loveliest blossom of all, large and open. *Cydonia oblonga* needs sun and warmth to ripen the fruit.

H: 15 ft (5 m); **S**: 15 ft (5 m)
❋❋❋ ◊ ◑ ☼

Echinacea purpurea "Augustkönigin"
The big, daisylike flowers of all the echinaceas are produced late in the summer and are insect-pollinated. "Augustkönigin" has strongly colored petals surrounding a large dark pincushion center. The central cone provides good winter interest.

H: 5 ft (1.5 m); **S**: 18 in (45 cm)
❋❋❋ ◊ ☼

Hebe "Amy"
This insect pollinated hebe grows slowly into a medium to large evergreen shrub. The dark green leaves can turn bronze in winter, and the large purple flowers are produced in late summer. If plants become overgrown, cut back hard.

H: 5 ft (1.5 m); **S**: 5 ft (1.5 m)
❋ ◊ ◑ ☼ ◑

Helenium "Sonnenwunder"
Heleniums are bold and impressive and flower over a long period in late summer. The insect-pollinated flowers can be found in shades of yellow, orange, red, and brown. Dig up and divide clumps every few years to keep the plant growing strongly.

H: 5 ft (1.5 m); **S**: 24 in (60 cm)
❋❋❋ ◊ ◑ ☼

Ilex x altaclerensis "Golden King"
The female forms of plants are of no risk to hayfever sufferers. *Ilex* "Golden King" is a female form, producing bright red berries to prove it. The foliage is golden variegated and almost entirely free of spines, and the plant's growth is compact.

H: 20 ft (6 m); **S**: 40–50 ft (12–15 m)
❄❄ ◊ ◑ ☼ ♛

Magnolia liliiflora "Nigra"
Like all magnolias, this small one is insect pollinated. It is a particularly beautiful form, with dark slender buds opening to deep purple-red flowers in May, which is usually late enough to avoid them being hit by spring frosts.

H: 10 ft (3 m); **S**: 8 ft (2.5 m)
❄❄❄ ◊ ☼ ♛

Malus
Crab apples have some of the showiest blossom of any tree and they are a beautiful addition to the spring garden (and insect pollinated). The blossom is followed by colorful fall fruits, which are held on the tree after the leaves fall.

H: 15–50 ft (5–15 m); **S**: 15–50 ft (5–15 m) ❄❄❄ ◊ ◑ ☼

Prunus
Peach is one of the genera *Prunus*, and like its close relatives—plum, damson, nectarine, apricot, cherry, and almond—is insect pollinated. Peaches need a warm, sheltered spot, preferably against a south-facing wall, if they are to thrive.

H: 5–70 ft (1.5–20 m); **S**: 5–70 ft (1.5–20 m) ❄❄❄ ◊ ◑ ☼

Rudbeckia fulgida var. sullivantii "Goldsturm"
This bold, insect-pollinated plant is one of the easiest perennials to grow, being short and neat enough to require no staking and only needing dividing occasionally. It produces its flowers late into the fall.

H: 36 in (90 cm); **S**: 18 in (45 cm)
❄❄❄ ◊ ☼ ◑ ♛

Verbena bonariensis
The vibrant purple, insect-pollinated flowers of *Verbena bonariensis* float above the herbaceous border. They are a color that seems to become increasingly vivid as light fades. Once settled, it seeds itself around the garden with abandon.

H: 6 ft (2 m); **S**: 18 in (45 cm)
❄❄ ◊ ◑ ☼ ♛

Index

Index

Acknowledgments

The publisher would like to thank the following for their kind permission to reproduce their photographs:

(Key: a-above; b-below/bottom; c-center; l-left; r-right; t-top)

2: Brian T. North, garden designed by Amanda Yorwerth. **6–7:** Marianne Majerus/MMGI: Grafton Cottage, Staffs. **8:** GAP Photos: J S Sira/Design: Kevin Scully, RHS Hampton Court Flower Show 2004. **9:** Marianne Majerus/MMGI: Design: LIz Inigo Jones (t), Clive Nichols: Design: Clare Matthews (c), Harpur Garden Library/Jerry Harpur: Design: Ryl Nowell (b). **10:** GAP Photos: Friedrich Strauss (br), Marianne Majerus/MMGI: (t) (bl). **11:** Steve Gunther. **13:** GAP Photos: Zara Napier (t), Jonathan Buckley/Design: Wendy & Leslie Howell (cl), Tim Gainey (br). **15:** Marianne Majerus/MMGI: Design: Jekka McVicar, RHS Chelsea 2000. **16:** GAP Photos: Zara Napier/Lucy Redman's School of Garden Design (t), Clive Nichols/ Design: Claire Matthews (b; **17:** Marianne Majerus/MMGI: Design: Tom Stuart-Smith (t). Design: Mary McCarthy (b). **18:** Marianne Majerus/MMGI. **20:** Elizabeth Whiting & Associates/www.ewastock.com (t), GAP Photos: Elke Borkowski (b). **21:** GAP Photos: Clive Nichols/Design: Clare Matthews (t). **22–23:** GAP Photos: Zara Napier. **24:** Marianne Majerus/MMGI: Design: Stuart Craine. **25:** GAP Photos: Clive Nichols/Design: Sarah Layton (t), John Glover (b). **26:** Marianne Majerus/ MMGI: Design: Nicola Gammon/www. shootgardening.co.uk (b). **27:** Elizabeth Whiting & Associates/www.ewastock.com (t), Marianne Majerus/MMGI: Design: Gardens and Beyond (b). **33:** GAP Photos: Jo Whitworth/Design: Del Buono Gazerwitz (br). **39:** GAP Photos: Geoff Kidd (br). **41:** GAP Photos: Richard Bloom (tl). **42:** Zara Napier (tl). **43:** Marianne Majerus/MMGI: Design: Ann Frith. **48–49:** Brian T. North. **62:** Marianne Majerus/ MMGI: Design: Bunny Guinness, The Herbalist Garden, RHS Chelsea 1998. **70–71:** Brian T. North. **74–75:** GAP Photos: Elke Borkowski. **76:** GAP Photos: J S Sira. **77:** Photolibrary: Howard Rice. **85:** Andrew Lawson: Design: The late Christopher Lloyd, Great Dixter. **87:** GAP Photos: John Glover. **89:** The Garden Collection: Derek Harris. **93:** GAP Photos: Lynn Keddie. **98–99:** GAP Photos: Leigh Clapp. **103:** GAP Photos: Dave Bevan (bl). **108:** Marianne Majerus/MMGI: Design: Diana Yakeley (br). **109:** GAP Photos: Leigh Clapp (tl),Clive Nichols/Design: Mark Gregory (bl); **110–111:** Marianne Majerus/ MMGI: Ashlie, Suffolk. **120:** David Murphy: (tc). **121:** David Murphy: (tr)

All other images © Dorling Kindersley For further information see: www.dkimages.com

Dorling Kindersley would also like to thank the following:

Index: Christine Bernstein Scott and Jane Orchard for the use of their allotment